CW01379051

WWW.
THE INTERNET.
COM

WWW.
THE INTERNET.
COM

Vicky Clark

CAXTON REFERENCE

© 2001 Caxton Editions

This edition published 2001 by Caxton Publishing Group Ltd,
20 Bloomsbury Street, London, WC1B 3QA.

Design and compilation by The Partnership Publishing Solutions Ltd,
Glasgow, G77 5UN

All rights reserved.
No part of this publication may be reproduced, stored in a retrieval
system, or transmitted, in any form or by any means, electronic,
mechanical, photocopying, recording or otherwise, without the prior
permission of the copyright holder.

Printed and bound in India

Contents

	Introduction	7
1	What is the Internet?	9
2	Now, let's begin!	27
3	Surfing the World Wide Web	39
4	Search Engines	49
5	Subject Directories	59
6	Other Databases	63
7	Meta Search Engines	71
8	Using Boolean Searches	79
9	On the Internet	87
10	What is E-mail?	109
11	Sending and Receiving E-mail	121
12	Using the WWW as a Teaching Tool	149
13	Starting and Designing your own WWW pages	161
14	Glossary	173
15	Frequently asked questions	217
16	Useful Websites	227

Introduction

Often, there are people who want to get on to the Internet but they have no idea just where to start or even how to use a computer in its most basic form. Other individuals are already on the Internet but they aren't really using it to its full advantage – they are not using of all of its features effectively, and therefore want to learn more.

The purpose of this book is to provide a starting point for each of those people and it will also guide them, and you, to the equipment and software which is necessary to use the Internet itself, and to fully take advantage of their Internet access. It will also help to provide plenty of information on how you can make the Internet work for you personally.

It will be assumed, in this guide, that you have very little knowledge of using a PC at all, so please bear with me if you feel you are more advanced than some of the points I am covering. This guide will therefore probably be of most benefit to those of you are totally new to the Internet.

It is worth bearing in mind that a great deal of this book is a glossary of terms that are used throughout this book and most others, including instruction manuals. So if, at any time, you feel that you do not understand what is being said, the glossary will explain the term, rather than you having to read of section of the book that you have just read all over again.

CHAPTER 1
What is the Internet?

What is the Internet?
If you really don't know what the Internet is, you are being honest – most people who don't know would not admit to it! A lot of people talk about the Internet as if everybody and his dog already know what it is, how it works and why it started. To put it in simple terms – this is really all you need to know – the Internet is basically a sprawling international network of computers. Nobody owns it. It was started years ago by scientists and government agencies that needed a quick and easy way to transfer vast amounts of data from one computer to another. The general public never knew it existed until a few things happened that transformed the Internet into the library and entertainment centre it has become today. One of the most important changes was that businesses started catching on, as they realised the potential that their business had through the

Internet. They, too, had lots of data to pass around to both customers and other businesses and other employees in a different location and they wanted to exploit that possibility. Once the Internet was open to business, the general public found out about it and the rest is history. The other major change that helped bring the Internet to people like you and me was the development of the World Wide Web, or WWW, which is the main way that people use the Internet. The World Wide Web is only a small part of the whole Internet, but without question its fastest growing part. To understand more about the WWW, it's helpful to understand how the whole Internet works, which is what will be explained in the next few sections. If you don't understand it all, don't worry too much because it is not a crucial part of being able to use the Internet, but it is useful to know a bit about its background.

Who can access the Internet?

Everyone! The Internet has been running for decades now, but the Net in its present form would never have been developed to such a high standard without the hundreds of unpaid voluntary efforts (as a matter of fact, the Internet is still mainly run on a voluntary basis). Everyone, with NO exception, has access to these new and developing forms of communication

What is the Internet?

technologies which are becoming more and more vital to participate actively in the events of our world. As more and more information is starting to become available online, many new doors open up for those who have access to that information. Unfortunately, unless such access is broadly encouraged among people from all walks of life, people will become discouraged and doors to the information can close.

What does 'Internet' actually mean?

The Internet is so-called because it is literally an INTERnational NETwork of computers which are all linked up. These networked computers then send all the information to your PC through your Internet service provider, or ISP. Confused? To put this in a more basic way, your personal computer can retrieve any information from what is called the Internet, because it is connected to a huge network of computers which have all banks of information stored in their memory. All these facts and figures mean that you can us the Internet to find answers to literally everything that you have ever wondered about, from famous people, to share prices, to ordering goods, to checking your bank balance. The Net also gives you the opportunity to listen to music and watch short video clips. It is also used in a major way in business. Small businesses and multinationals alike use the Internet as a means of attracting new business, to communicate with current clients and to renew contracts and build up successful working relationships. It also allows for the advertising and marketing of new and existing products and services. All major banks and building societies are now online, so even banking and other financial transactions can be carried out on the Internet.

But what is the Internet?

The Internet consists of the world wide web and also e-mail, which is a means of typing a message for someone and it being instantly sent to them. In other words, the world wide web and the Internet are not technically the same thing, although many people refer to them as being one and the same.

The world wide web is the tool that we use to find and search for information that we may need, and it will be done in a much easier way that would be achieved by going to a library. The Internet, however, is much more than this, and we will have a thorough look at everything that the Net consists of later on in this book.

The Internet has developed at an amazing rate but to achieve everything that businesses and consumers hope it will one day provide, a vast

What is the Internet?

amount of further development needs to be carried out. The system we currently use has definite limits. For one, there are now so many people using the Internet, that the speed we retrieve information from the Net is actually slowing down, rather than speeding up and becoming more efficient, hence keeping up with technology.

There are also many problems with Internet service providers being so busy at certain times of the day that no more users can have any access at all until less people are logged on again. We are entering the age of digital technology, but the Net is now having to play catch-up with this. A lot has to be achieved before the Net will be close to being fully digital. At the moment, a large proportion of the information on the Net is American, which can be frustrating for users, depending on the type of information that they are searching for. However, if you are looking for advice or facts regarding a specific company or town, for example, there shouldn't be any problem at all in finding this.

Now for the serious (and more boring!) bit... The Internet is made up of thousands of different communities – you cannot visit any of them, except through your computer keyboard. Their highways are wires and optical fibres; their language a series of ones and zeroes. Your PC is the only way you can access this information. These communities of cyberspace are as real and vibrant as any you could find on a globe or in an atlas. If anything, they are MORE real, as you can access three-dimensional views of places, instead of looking at a flat map on a piece of paper, for instance. The people who program the computers are just like us – not necessarily professionals, not necessarily college-educated, but they have a desire to learn about various topics and to share their interests with al of us too. There are real people on the other sides of those monitors. And freed from physical limitations, these people are developing new types of communities – ones which are defined more by common interest and purpose than by where they live or were born – ones on which what really counts is what you say and think and feel, not how you look or talk or how old you are. This may sound like a very politically correct way to look at the Internet, but it is in fact true. Anyone can write about anything – religion can be discussed by those of another religion, and the reader may not even know this. It removes some of the barriers and prejudices that TV or newspapers may not be able to avoid. Another example of this is if a famously right-wing newspaper was to write an article on the Labour Party, it would instantly be taken to be a prejudiced article when, in fact, it may be 100% factual. If, however, the same article appeared independently on the Net, it may be seen

What is the Internet?

as being a very balanced and fair piece of writing.

The most developed of these communities who are now using the world wide web is that of the scientists, which actually predates computers by a long chalk. Scientists have long seen themselves as an international community, where ideas were more important than their national origin. It is not surprising that the scientists were the first to adopt the new electronic media as their principal means of day-to-day communication.

One day in the not-too distant future, we will all – not just scientists – be able to enjoy the similar benefits of a truly global community.

But how does a community grow out of a computer network?

It does so because the network in turn enables new forms of communication. The most obvious example of these new digital communications media is electronic mail, but there are many others. We should begin to think of mailing lists, news groups, file and document archives, etc. as just the first generation of new forms of information and communications media. All of these will be discussed to some extent throughout this book.

The digital media of computer networks, because of their design and the technology upon which they ride, are vastly different from the now dominant mass media of television, radio, newspapers and magazines. Digital communications media are capable of being much more interactive, more participatory, more decentralised, and less hierarchical. As such, the types of social relations and communities which can be built on these media share these characteristics. Computer networks encourage the active participation of individuals rather than the passive non-participation encouraged by television. In mass media, the vast majority of participants are passive recipients of information – they simply watch TV, read a newspaper, listen to a radio. In digital communications media, however, the vast majority of participants are active creators of information as well as recipients. This type of symmetry has previously only been found in media like the telephone, where both parties involved have equal opportunity to talk and input information. But while the telephone is almost entirely a medium for private one-to-one communication, computer network applications such as electronic mailing lists, conferences and bulletin boards, serve as a medium of group or "many-to-many" communication, allowing more than two people to participate at any one time. In fact, there can be hundreds of people involved in a chat at one time.

The new forums on computer networks are the

What is the Internet?

great levellers and reducers of organisational hierarchy. Each user has, at least in theory, access to every other user, and an equal chance to be heard. Some US high-tech companies, such as Microsoft and Borland, already use this to good advantage. Their directors are directly accessible to every single one of their employees via their internal electronic mail system. This creates a sense that the voice of the individual employee really does matter. More generally, when corporate communication is allowed by electronic mail, decision-making processes can be far more inclusive and participatory. There are occasions where companies may offer an incentive to their employees to come up with money-saving techniques which would benefit the company. E-mail allows this to be done quickly, and any possible solutions are received from the employees instantly. This also gives the employees a sense of greater importance – the manager directly e-mailed them to ask for help – they didn't simply put a poster on the wall for everyone to read.

Computer networks do not require tightly centralised administrative control. In fact, decentralisation is an advantage and is necessary to enable rapid growth of the network itself. Tight controls will simply serve to kill off any new growth. This decentralisation promotes the sense of inclusion, as it lowers barriers to entry for new parties wishing to join the network. All of these characteristics of using computer networks show that networks have the potential add to and encourage cultural, political, and social lives.

The Internet and related networks represent a great example of a computer network with all of the qualities discussed above. It is an open network of networks, not a single, stand alone network, but a mixture of interconnected systems which operate on multiple implementations of accepted protocols and standards. One of the important features of the Internet is that new networks, host systems, and users may readily join the network – it is open to all.

The accessibility of the Internet reflects the values and opinion of the people who write and program it. Future generations will owe an awful lot to this community for the wisdom of building these types of open and accessible systems. However, it can be said that the fundamental qualities of the Net, such as its decentralisation discussed above, also pose problems. What about software bugs that bring down computers, or other users who try to do the same? The problems can and will be solved, whether permanently or on a developing level.

Reaching the public
The Internet can be used in many ways, but an

What is the Internet?

incident using Ross Perot's 1992 Presidential campaign is worth using as an example of the affect the Internet can have on reaching the public. His idea was to have something called an "electronic town meeting". Perot's idea, from 20 years or so ago, was that viewers would watch a debate on television and fill out opinion and question cards, which would be mailed in and collated. We could now do it with hundreds of telephone numbers by using the medium of the Internet. This has been adapted further to create online debating. This allows the inclusion of multiple active participants, not just experts, which will help to represent every point of view, in discussions that unfold over long periods of time.

What this shows is that, far from being alienated and disaffected from the political process, people will talk and discuss any policies if they have the opportunity to do so. Mass media don't allow anything like that to happen.

Talk turns to action on the net

In 1987, the Federal Communications Commission proposed changing the way certain online providers paid for their access to local phone service. Online, this quickly became known as the "modem tax" and it succeeded in generating a storm of protest. The

FCC withdrew the idea, but not quickly enough. The "modem tax" has now penetrated so deeply into the core of the Net that it has taken up a permanent residence as a kind of virtual virus, which periodically causes a re-infection of the systems and its users. FCC commissioners continue to receive substantial mail on this even though the original issue died a long time ago. In fact, it has – and still does – generate more mail than any other issue in the history of the FCC.

More recently, the chairman of Lotus Development Corporation in the States, Jim Manzi, received more than 30,000 e-mail messages when the company was getting ready to sell a database containing records on tens of millions of Americans. There was a huge flood of e-mailed complaints about the threat to privacy helped force the company to abandon the project. Issues of little but vital interest to the online community therefore give a guide as to how strong the organising power of the Net can be. Another example of the power of the Net, and its importance of being completely up to date, was in August, 1991. The managers of a Soviet computer network known as Relcom stayed online during a coup, and they relayed eye witness accounts and news of actions which were taken against the coup to the West and to the rest of Russia. There were hundreds of people linked to this update at the time, to keep an eye on the up to the second reporting. Many public interest non-profit organisations and special interest groups already use such bulletin boards heavily as a way to communicate among their members and to organise political activity.

But everything is not yet perfect online. The quality of such discussions can be and is often very low. The discussions which take place are often very trivial and boring and lacking any real persuasive opinion or even reason. The discussion can often turn to remarks which are insulting and amount to being personal attacks, instead of continuing with serious and informative discussion. It is also common for some individuals who are taking part in any of the discussions to dominate the conversation and this is simply because they have time to do so. It turns the debate into an unbalanced and unfair discussion and a lot of the valid points that are being made are lost in the mass of input from those with not much to say. There is a place on the Internet for serious discussion, but if you wish to join in a balanced debate, it is best if it is being regulated by a body of people, so that the comments are screened before they are included,. This means that there will be no meaningless or worthless comments appearing in the debate. Information overload can also be a problem. There is usually simply far too much in each conversation and in each subject that appears on the Internet to read to keep up with. It is, in many areas, without any real organisation.

Some of these problems have to do with the unrefined and very basic design and structure of the discussion medium itself. The stream of new messages are simply added to the screen and appear in columns of text. This can begin to create a kind of hypnotic trance. This is one part of the Internet that does not yet compare with the various type fonts, layouts, diagrams and pictures which we can see on the printed page. BUT it still comes back to the interactive advantage of the Internet and that the net can be updated in seconds if new information comes in - a newspaper cannot. Many key inventions are occurring slowly, for example, with the development of software tools that will allow the publication of audio and video across the Net. This type of software has usually been done so far by volunteers who have given away the results. It's a great thing to be developed, but it's not as yet sufficient, given how hard it is to develop good software.

Overloading on the Internet

There are problems with certain features of the Internet. E-mail is overloaded because there aren't readily available alternatives yet. New and different kinds of tools are needed for work which allows us

What is the Internet?

to work together. Computer conferencing, as it develops and grows, may actually be enough for carrying out discussion and debate. But, at the moment, it cannot by itself really support group work, in the sense of allowing a group to make decisions efficiently, and to represent and track the status of its work process.

Trying to run an organisation via e-mail mailing list is very different than trying to have a discussion. It is unlikely that one will completely replace the other for some time or, at least, until new software is developed. Computer networks can only fully realise their potential as innovative communications media in an environment which encourages free and open expression. In some countries, legal principles of free speech protect freedom of expression in traditional media such as the printed word. But once communication moves to new digital media and crosses international borders, these legal protections fall away completely. There is no internationally binding legal authority which protects free expression on national networks. There are guidelines, but they are not yet legally binding.

Because the medium is so new, it is important now to develop policies at the national and international level that help achieve the potential of computer networks for society as a whole. By the time television was recognised as a vast wasteland it was already too late to change. There is a rare opportunity to develop policies in advance of a technologically and economically mature system which would be hard to change. Both broadcast and cable TV were introduced with similar fanfare. The results have been disappointing. Because of regulatory failure and the limits of the technology, they failed to be saviours of education or political life as it was implied they might be. TV is something that is well loved and very, very popular but most people know and recognise that it is largely a cultural wasteland an much of it is simply for entertainment purposes. However, digital TV services are now allowing a much more interactive way to watch and communicate through your TV. None of the interactive services will be possible, however, if we have a vast superhighway running into each and every home and only a narrow footpath coming back out. Instead of settling for a multimedia version of the same entertainment that is increasingly dissatisfying on today's TV, we really need a superhighway that encourages the production and distribution of a broader, wider range of programming. The superhighway should be required to provide so-called open platform services. In today's channel-based cable TV system, program producers must negotiate for channel space with cable companies around the country. In an open platform network, we would avoid that bottleneck from occurring. Every person would have access to the entire superhighway, so programmers could distribute information directly to consumers. Consumers would in fat become producers – individuals and small organisations could create and distribute programs to anyone on the highway who wants them. Open platform services will help to increase diversity in the electronic media, just as low production and distribution costs make possible a wide variety of newspapers and magazines.

Although the previous section may be boring, it is useful to know a bit about the background to current debates that exist regarding the Internet. It is always an advantage to know the basics of anything before you learn how to use it in more detail.

Chapter 2
Now, let's begin!

Welcome to the Internet! You are about to learn how to travel and navigate through a unique land without frontiers, a place that is everywhere at once! You'll be joining a community of millions of people – growing more and more each day – around the world who use this global resource on a daily basis.

With this book, you will learn how to use the Internet to:
- communicate and stay in touch with friends, relatives and colleagues around the world, at a tiny fraction of the cost of phone calls or even mailing a letter
- discuss anything and everything from archaeology to zoology with up to hundreds of people in several different languages
- access thousands of information databases and libraries world-wide
- retrieve any of thousands of documents, journals,

books and computer programs and games
- stay up to date with news and sports and also with official weather reports – all from all over the world
- play live, "real time" games with dozens of other people at once
- download new software or new computer games.

You will be one of the newest members of this ever growing and ever loved group of people. If you become a regular user of the Net, you will learn about things you didn't even know existed and you will learn much more about subjects that you thought you were an expert on! It is good fun to use the Internet – as well as very useful and educational – but you may not take to all of it immediately, so it is worthwhile to have an open mind about it and remember –- don't get too stressed about any of it!

Can't I just do these things in a library?
Technically – and on a basic level – yes, you can. But the Net has many benefits, which include allowing information to be updated literally instantly if there are any new facts or theories that have come to light. It also has the great advantage of its pages being updated by so many different people from various walks of life that there are diverse opinions as well as

Now, let's begin!

hard facts.

There are disadvantages to using the Internet, however. One of the disadvantages of using information that you have found on the Net is that it is not always checked carefully and thoroughly by a professional body, so the information that you are using may not, in fact, be 100% reliable or factual.

However, we now have the best of both worlds – many encyclopaedias and dictionaries are now accessible online, so we have access to huge amounts of factual information which is being updated regularly and is being adapted should the opportunity arise.

How and why did the Internet begin?

The Internet began over 30 years ago, and was initially conceived and developed by the American Defence Department. The original point of it was to be used as a way of communicating any important information and intelligence quickly and securely. Then, in the 1980s, other networks began to join and began to develop the Net as we know it today.

These days, it is very easy to find somewhere local that will rent you some Internet time. It is not expensive to do this – some companies are charging as little as £1 per hour to use their PCs. You therefore don't need to have your own PC, or the use of a friend's, to be able to use the Net. Internet cafes are available in most major cities, and local libraries also generally have PCs that are connected to the Internet. If, however, you would prefer to be online from home, most PC shops sell kits which have everything you need to be connected almost immediately. There are also other options, such as Internet TV and digital TV, that offer e-mail facilities. E-mail phones are also available. The disadvantage of all of them, however, is that they will simply offer you e-mail or Internet facilities, but will not give you the option of using other PC packages, such as Word, Excel etc.. PCs are becoming more and more affordable as technology develops and their popularity grows. If you are a complete beginner to the world of PCs, it might be a good idea to go to an Internet cafe to begin with, so that you can then decide if you want to commit to spending a large sum of money on a PC. It also means that there are people working there who are paid to get you started and to help you through any teething problems you might have. This will make the whole experience of going online much less daunting than if you were at home with a large user manual, trying to plough your way slowly through something that is really a foreign language.

Do I need lots of equipment and software?

The whole world – and everything in it – is just one short phone call away. With a computer and modem, you'll be able to connect to the Internet, the world's largest computer network If you are very lucky, you won't even need the modem because many colleges and companies now allow their students or employees to have direct access to the Internet. The phone line can be your existing voice line, but if you have any extensions, you (and everybody else in the house or office) won't be able to use them for voice calls while you are connected to the Net, as using the Net causes the line to become engaged.

The first, and arguably most important, thing that you are going to need to connect to the Internet is a fast modem – as fast as you can afford. It is worth spending more money on the modem and slightly less on the PC itself, as the modem will determine how fast any information you are looking for will be sent to you.

The modem is what determines the rate at which you will be able to retrieve requested information from the Net. A modem is a sort of translator between computers and the phone system. It is needed because computers and the phone system process and transmit lots of data, or information, in two different and incompatible ways.

Computers talk to each other digitally, that is,

they store and process information as a series of discrete numbers. The phone network, however, relies on analogue signals, which look and act like a series of waves. When your computer is ready to transmit data to another computer over a phone line, your modem acts as a converter. It changes the computer numbers into these analogue waves, which sound like a lot of screeching. In other words, it modulates them. In turn, when information waves come into your modem, it converts them into numbers your computer can process, by demodulating them.

Increasingly, computers come with modems already installed. If yours didn't, you'll have to decide on what speed of modem to get. Modem speeds are judged in "BPS rate" or bits per second. One BPS means the modem can transfer roughly one bit per second. In other words, the greater the BPS rate, the more quickly a modem can send and receive information. Every letter or character is made up of eight bits. You can now buy a 2400-BPS modem for well under £50, and most even come with the ability to handle fax messages as well. At prices that now start around £120, you can buy a modem that can transfer data at 14,400 BPS (and often even faster, if you use special compression techniques). If you think you might be using the Net to transfer large numbers of files, a faster modem is always worth the

Now, let's begin!

price. It will dramatically reduce the amount of time your modem or computer is tied up transferring files and, if you are paying for Net access by the hour, will save you quite a lot of money in online charges.

Like the computer to which it attaches, a modem is useless without software to tell it how to work. Most modems today come with easy-to-install software. Try the program out. If you find it difficult to use or understand, consider going to your local software shop to find a better program. You can spend hundreds of pounds on a communications program, but unless you have very specialised needs, this will be a waste of money, as there are lots of excellent programs available for around £80 or less.

Among the basic features you want to look for are a choice of different "protocols", which will be explained more later, for transferring files to and from the Net and it should also have the ability to write script or command files that allow you to automate such steps as logging into a host system. When you buy a modem and the software, make sure you ask the dealer how to install and use them — they may do this for you as part of the service. Try out the software first before buying if you can. If the dealer can't help you, find another dealer. It is their job to help you, so they should help you!

To fully take advantage of the Net, it is recommended that you spend a few minutes going over the manuals or documentation that comes with your software, as well as simply reading this book. There may be various features that your PC comes with that are not covered in this book. Also, because of the speed that software and hardware is being developed, things may even have changed slightly from when this was written. There are a few things you should pay special attention to – uploading and downloading; screen capturing or screen dumping; logging; how to change protocols; and terminal emulation. It is also essential to know how to convert a file which has been created by your word processing program into "ASCII" or "text" format, which will then let you share any of your thoughts with others across the Net.

Uploading is the process of sending a file from your computer to a system on the Net. Downloading is retrieving a file from somewhere on the Net to your computer. In general, things in cyberspace go "up" to the Net and come "down" to you. All of these features will be discussed, so don't panic if this is all coming at you too quickly!

The chances are your software will come with a choice of several "protocols" to use for these transfers. These protocols are systems designed to ensure that line noise or static does not cause errors that could ruin whatever information you are trying to transfer. Essentially, when using a protocol, you

Now, let's begin!

are transferring a file in a series of pieces. After each piece is sent or received, your computer and the Net system compare it. If the two pieces don't match exactly, they transfer it again, until they agree that the information they both have is identical. If, after several tries, the information just doesn't make it across, you'll either get an error message or your screen will freeze. In that case, try it again. If, after five tries, you are still stuck, something is wrong with either the file, the telephone line, the system you're connected to or your own computer.

The second item you will need is to have a good world wide web browser, such as Internet Explorer or Netscape. Internet Explorer is the most popular in the UK. The explosion of the World wide web over the last couple of years has given the Internet the huge popularity that it has today. The World wide web allows you to access information on almost any subject imaginable with only a few keystrokes. Your world wide web browser is the centre piece of your Internet software.

Finally, you will need to have an account with an Internet Service Provider, also known as an ISP. This is the company that will connect you to the Internet each time you wish to use it. The ISP is therefore the company who will decide how much you will be charged when you are connected. It is therefore very worth while checking them thoroughly before you start to use one.

Many ISPs give away disks which allow you to try them out for a set period of time, often free of charge for this period. The disks also often give you incentives to connect to the ISP. Once you have an account with an Internet Service Provider, it is useful, if not necessary, to have software that allows you to connect your computer straight to the Internet, and as quickly as possible, by dialling your service provider. If you have Windows 95, or any Windows program after '95, you will not need to buy or install any additional programs, as it is ready and able to carry out your dial-up networking needs and it will therefore be used instead of any dial-up program.

Once you have an account with an ISP, you will need to set up your PC so that it is compatible with the account, and so that the ISP recognises your account each time you try to connect to the Internet. The set-up of each ISP is very different for every service provider, so I would recommend that you check the home page of your ISP carefully to ensure that you set up your PC correctly.

Which modem should I use?

There are 2 main types of modem that can be used to connect you to the Net – internal and external

Now, let's begin!

modems.

Internal modems are the most popular choice for most PC users, mainly because they are considerably cheaper than internal modems. The downside to this, however, is that they are also much slower at retrieving information from the Internet. Internal modems plug into a socket inside the computer itself. This therefore involves taking the back off your PC and following step by step instructions to install it correctly. Otherwise, the store where you bought it will be able to install it for you, or you may be lucky and already have one fitted as standard. They are usually the best option for PCs at home, as they are fitted inside the casing of the computer itself and so they don't take up any extra workspace and they don't need any additional power source. The downside is that they are slower than external modems.

On the other hand, an external modem is much easier to install. It plugs into the bag of your PC, which means that they are easy to upgrade if you wish to buy or install a newer or more powerful modem in the future. They are also easy to interchange between PCs. The disadvantage of an external modem is that they require an additional source of power – either a car battery or a power socket.

What you need – in brief

To connect to the Internet, you will therefore need three things – a computer, a modem and an Internet service provider, commonly known as an ISP. There are obviously many more attachments and accessories that *can* be fitted but, to begin with, these three items are all that are absolutely necessary for you to find information on the Net. They don't need to be the most advanced or powerful models on the market but, if they are basic models, the speed at which the information will be retrieved will be comparatively slower than more advanced ones.

The modem is the main factor which will affect this. If you have a slow and not very powerful modem, a powerful PC will have a lot of wasted potential, so it is best to invest more to have the most powerful, and therefore fastest, modem you can afford.

CHAPTER 3
Surfing the World Wide Web

More and more these days, you will see adverts and promotions on almost everything you can buy which have a little sign advising you to look at **www.something** on the Internet. This is known as a world wide web site address and it will allow you to find further information on the company or product on the world wide web. They allow you to access the usable friendly face of the Internet and will often give you information on the company and will usually give you the chance to e-mail the company with comments or questions you may have about them or their products or services.

Once you learn how to use the world wide web, you will find out how easy it is to access all that varied and useful information that is available to each and every one of us out there. The world wide web itself allows such vast freedom of expression that it has sparked off a revolution in publishing, both by amateurs and recognised authors, that it is unmatched at any other time in history.

Scrolling

Some world wide web pages, like many Word and Excel are too long to fit on your screen. Many of you will already know how to scroll the screen, so that you can see the rest of the text, but some of you won't, and there's not much point in knowing all about the web and how to use it if you don't know how to move down a page! So that you don't miss out on everything which lies at the bottom of the page, you should find a scroll bar on the right hand side. It is the long thin vertical line which runs down the very right hand side of your screen, whether it be on a Word document or the Internet. There is a small arrow which points upwards at the top and one pointing down at the bottom. If you use your mouse to position your cursor (the little white arrow that you can move around your screen) onto the little box at the bottom which has the arrow on it, and click a few times, you should find that the whole page moves upwards, i.e. allowing you to see what is further down the page. To move the page back down again, carry out the same process by using the arrow at the top of the scroll bar. Another way of moving the page up and down is by using the 'block' which

Surfing the World Wide Web

appears on the scroll bar. It will be found somewhere between the two "arrow" boxes you've just used. If you move your cursor so that it points to this block and click and hold the mouse button down, when you slide it up and down, the page should move too.

You have now worked out how to move around the actual page you are looking at, so you are ready to learn how to begin searching the web.

Copying words and pictures from the Internet

As before, this works in the same way as it would if you were copying some information from a Word document. The only difference being that there are Copyright rules similar to those in most types of publishing that are enforced on the Internet.

All you have to do is highlight the section of text or the picture that you wish to copy. You do this by pointing the cursor to the point where you want your copying to begin, click the left button on your mouse and keep it pressed in, then drag the cursor down to the very end of the area you wish to copy. This will highlight the area in black. Now, while the cursor is pointing to any part of the highlighted area, click the right button of the mouse. It will give you the options of cut, copy or paste. At this stage, you will be unable to cut the section (as it is impossible for you to alter a web page) so click on "copy". Then all you have to do is go to the Word document (or similar) where you wish it to be transferred to, click the cursor into the position you wish it to begin and right click on the mouse. Now click on "paste" and all the information you copied will miraculously appear!

Browsing
To begin to access any of the information available to you, you need to learn how to browse the world wide web. To do this, you will need to connect and set up a world wide web browser to your PC. This is the tool that is used to get you to any of the sites that you wish to see. These sites cover a vast range of topics, such as music, investment companies, banks, museums, art galleries, radio stations, movie trailers and a whole lot more.

The world wide web, in fact, currently has information on more than 10 million companies and is accessed by more than 300 million users if the Internet. Due to the easy accessibility of all this information, this will increase rapidly all the time. The browser that you use will get you to the information you want to find and will bring it to you whilst you sit at your keyboard pressing a few buttons. No dictionary or encyclopaedia can or ever will match the information the world wide web can

Surfing the World Wide Web

give you, and the best part of it is that much of it is free to access!

Visiting a world wide web site can be done in various ways. The first way to do this can be done if you know the what is known as a world wide web address. All you have to do is submit the address to your browser by clicking on a link or by typing an address by hand. An address bar runs horizontally across the top of your world wide web browser screen on your monitor. When it is blank, there will be the prompt to "go to". When an address has been entered, the wording changes to "location" or "net site" on Netscape based servers. Microsoft Internet explorer says simply "address". If you know the address of the world wide web site you wish to access, simply type it into the address bar, hit ENTER and then wait. The address which you have submitted will be examined by your world wide web browser and will be checked to make sure it is a legitimate address. If it is, the world wide web browser will then contact your local DNS server and will then convert the address to an IP address. While this is happening, if you look at the bottom left-hand corner of your screen, you will see a message which shows you that the address is being converted. Once it has been converted, the browser contacts the world wide web site's server and will then retrieve and display the pages which are available on that world wide web site.

Confused? To put it in a much simpler way, all you really need to know at this stage is that if you type in a known world wide web address into the address bar at the top of the Internet screen, your browser will carry out all the necessary actions to allow that Internet site to appear on your screen so you can look through it. If the address you typed in is correct, the page will be retrieved for you and you can look through it thoroughly. If it does not connect however, check the address you have entered is correct and try again. If the address was correct, there may simply have been a minor fault that stopped the connection the first time, but when you try again it should work.

But what is a World Wide Web site?

If you are on the Internet and you enter a world wide web address on your world wide web browser, the page that you requested will be retrieved from wherever it may be stored on the Internet itself. The world wide web browser then displays the world wide web site on your screen in front of you for you to access.

World wide web pages themselves are pages of information relating to a specific subject or company, for instance. An example of this is if you entered the

Surfing the World Wide Web

world wide web address www.bbc.co.uk, the page that would appear in front of you would be the index page for the BBC and would then give you the chance to search further by looking at details on today's news, or on any of the departments of the BBC and will even allow you to check if there are any jobs available within the company. World wide web pages, then, are usually a mix of text and images (which could be diagrams, drawings, photos etc. etc.) in a semi-magazine type format.

All world wide web pages contain links to other information stored in that site, and there are often links which will take you to a completely different world wide web address that is linked in some way to the information you are looking at. For instance, on the BBC news page, you may be able to then go straight to news headlines on other world wide web sites. To access one of these links, all you have to do is to move your mouse until the cursor points at the link, and then click on it. Something will happen after a few seconds. Clicking on these links will help you to navigate round the world wide web, and is much simpler than you having to type an address in full each time you wish to look at something else. Simply, clicking on a link is like turning the page of a book. To explain this in technical terms, the reason that the links can be used is that all world wide web pages are written and programmed in hyper text mark-up language, or HTML. This language allows the document to link straight to another document without the need to start all over again from scratch.

Depending on how you have set up your world wide web browser, text which allows you to link to other documents will either be highlighted in a different colour or will be underlined, which allows them to be easily seen if your scanning through the text. As well as these two forms of highlighting the links, if you pass over a link using the mouse, the cursor will change from an arrow symbol to a hand with a pointing finger which points to the link itself. To connect to the highlighted page, simply use your mouse to point the cursor at the link and click the mouse on it. This will lead the browser to the appropriate link. It is worth remembering that links to other pages are actually one-way connections. This means that it could be taken that if you lick around for a while, that you'll eventually end up lost on the Internet. It could, however, also mean that you may in fact end up back where you started! There are however many techniques that could be used to get back without too many problems. These will be discussed as we continue through the book.

If your PC is equipped with a 56K modem, the normal time taken for world wide web pages to transmit is around 30 seconds or so. The revolutionary new service, known as broad band connection, can give an almost instantaneous connection.

Chapter 4
Search Engines

The use of a search engine

Now that you have got a world wide web browser and have set up an account with an ISP, you will need to learn how to use them effectively to find information easily and quickly on the world wide web. This is what a Search Engine is used for. A search engine can be described as a tool that crawls around the world wide web as you direct it, and it will remember everywhere it has been and everything you have looked at accurately and exactly. It will find and therefore allow you to retrieve information which is based on key words and prompts that that you give to it.

A search engine is arguably the easiest way to find something on the net, because it means that you don't have to know a specific world wide web address to link to it. Until now, you have probably been wondering how you will ever find anything on the millions of web sites and pages you can access. Well, a search engine will help you to find anything you wish to look for.

There are many search engines that can be used, for example Alta Vista, Google, Yahoo, Excite and Lycos. Each search engine has good points and bad points but, really, they are all fairly similar to use and you will be able to work out which you prefer after you have used each of them a few times.

Search engines do not incur any additional charges to your Internet service – they are simply part of the Internet itself and, as such, they are simply usable at the normal rate your ISP charges (if anything at all). I will now explain the basic guidelines of how to use a search engine and how to use it effectively and efficiently.

How do I use a search engine?

How to find things on the Internet and on the world wide web is going to be the basic and key skill that you will need to have if you wish to use the Internet to any extent at all. If you do not have this basic skill, you may find yourself ploughing through pages and pages of information that are of no use to you before you find what you are looking for, so it is important to read this section thoroughly and make sure you are familiar with it. You may like to hear,

Search Engines

though, that it is a fairly easy and straightforward tool to learn, so it shouldn't take too long to understand. It is also worth noting at this point that, in today's day and age, it is almost a necessity to have some sort of Internet skills – even the most basic – to be employable at all, so if you are skilled in this field, you will in fact be desirable in a place of employment. This chapter will at least give you enough knowledge to wok out your own system of finding things and browsing the world wide web, which is a good starting point for any user.

A search engine is the name given to the page that will allow you to search the world wide web effectively. It is, in fact, a database of world wide web pages and world wide web sites which have been gathered and put together to allow you to quickly access the information you are looking for. In other words, it is simply an index of various world wide web sites that have been put together to allow browsing the world wide web to be an easy task. A search engine will enable you to find a specific subject or even a specific word that is mentioned in world wide web pages. Basically, all you have to do is to type in the word or subject you wish to find out about, and the search engine will pull out all the world wide web pages and sites in its index and will bring up a list of all the sites that have a match. Obviously, because you may be looking for something specific, the suggestions the browser gives you may not be what you are looking for, so it is worth searching again but adding another word that may narrow down what you are looking for. To make this clearer, an example would be if you typed in the phrase pop music. The engine may bring up a list of hundreds of sites on pop music, pop groups, music magazines, music catalogues, music shops, and the list goes on. However, you could search again, but by refining the search by changing it to 1970s pop music. This may then bring up a list of options for you to search, such as 70s pop groups, music TV programmes, etc.. to refine it even further, you could change your key words to 1970s pop music CDs. This would then make the list of options even fewer, by only bringing up a list of options such as shops or on-line services where you can buy CDs which feature pop music or pop groups of the 1970s. in other words, when you are going to search for something by using a search engine, it is the database that is being searched and not the world wide web itself.

Each engine has a program running on it which means that it is constantly looking for new world wide web pages and world wide web sites that are not stored on it, and it also looks for any sites that have had their address changed or have new links attached to them. This allows the database to be

Search Engines

updated all the time.

Each search engine is similar in that there will be a box for you to type in the key words, and then they will produce a list of links that will relate to these words in some way. There will also be a note telling you how many links that have been discovered, for example "results 1-12 of 216" would mean that there were 12 links on that page, but a total of 216 possible links had been found by the search engine. Each result on the list will consist of a top line which tells you the name of the world wide web page or the world wide web site. There will then be a few lines which describe what the page consists of, or an extract from the site itself. If the link looks as if it is suitable to find any appropriate information, then you just click on that link and you will be taken there in less than a minute, usually.

A tip at this point, which many skilled users of the Net don't know about, is that the best way to search through a list of possible sites your browser has given you is to hold the SHIFT key while you click on the link. This will allow you to actually open the link as a new window, so if it doesn't have any information you need, you can either minimise or close that window. This saves a lot of time compared to the way many people check the sites – by clicking on a link and then clicking on "back" if it is no good.

As previously mentioned, all search engines work

in a similar way, but some are much more effective than others. This means that you should try a few and make sure that the one you use most often is efficient and has plenty of information open to you.

A closer look at Yahoo!

Description
Yahoo! (http://www.yahoo.com) is a human-compiled subject directory and a commercial portal. It is the oldest major directory and search engine on the world wide web, launched in mid-1994, and is a good starting point for information of general appeal.

Recently Yahoo! partnered with Google in order to provide World wide web page matches for search terms falling outside the boundaries of Yahoo! sites and categories.

Finally, according to *Wired* – a US-based magazine, Yahoo! is now accepting pay for placement of commercial world wide web sites in lists of results.

Yahoo! searches in;
- Its own subject directory
- The World wide web and provides secondary results via Google.

Search Engines

Yahoo! supports;
Searches in Yahoo's subject categories
(defaulting to Google for world wide web searches)
Implied Boolean (+) and (-) signs
Double quotes (" ") for phrases
Field searching of title (t:) and URL (u:)

Google supports;
Implied Boolean (+) and (-) signs
Double quotes (" ") for phrases
Field searching of title (t:) and URL (u:)
Boolean-type searching with radio buttons
("all" = AND; "any" = OR; "exact phrase match" and "Intelligent default")
Yahoo subject category searches
Google world wide web searches
Usenet news groups searches
Date range searches, from 1 day to 4 years
Results displayed, from 20 to 100
Special features they have;
    Topic and region-specific Yahoos!
    Automatic truncation
    No case sensitivity
    No stop words

If you've ever used a search service to find something on the World wide web, you know it is not nearly as effective as your local library's card catalogue. For instance, if you search for football, hoping to find some information about forthcoming professional tournaments, you may end up with a link to someone's page about an amateur club that he coaches. You could obviously improve things by adding or altering your key words you have used in your search, but it isn't all your fault! Searches can be useless for many reasons - some of them are fairly innocent, some less so. firstly, there's no single governing body to control and index the Internet the way libraries catalogue books under the Dewey System. There are many ways that can be used to search the web. There are more than a dozen search services and hundreds of more specialised ones. The problem is also added to with the fact that each new search engine arrives with its own way of doing things. Search sites are trying to make the best of this mess, but they may not be telling you everything you need to know. The truth is, the sites that appear at the top of the list when you do a search are not always sites that have anything at all to do with your search. On one hand, the way many search engines index pages leaves loopholes that allow eager web writers to add the most used key words to their web site, causing their sites to appear higher on the list of results when you search via a particular key word. On the other hand, all of the search engines are obviously companies which are there to make a

Search Engines

profit, and some have been entering into deals with content providers and advertisers that could compromise the unbiased nature of their listings.

CHAPTER 5
Subject Directories

What are subject directories?
Subject directories, unlike search engines, are created and maintained by human writers and editors and not by electronic robots and programs. The editors will review and then select sites which they feel should be included and added to their directories and indexes. This decision is usually made beforehand – i.e. they are given a list of features or subjects that site must contain if it is to be included. This may be simply that it is a .co.uk site. Their directories tend to be smaller than search engine databases and will often only index the home page or top level pages of a site.

How do subject directories work?
When you begin a key word search of a directory's contents, the directory will try to match your key

words and phrases with those in its written descriptions. Subject directories come in many different styles – there are general directories, academic directories, commercial directories, portals, and now, vortals. Portals are directories that have been created or taken over by commercial companies and are then changed to act as gateways to the world wide web. The portal sites do not only link to the popular subject categories, they also offer additional services such as e-mail, current news, stock quotes, travel information and maps.

Vortals, or vertical portals are subject-specific directories, as opposed to the broader, more generalised range of subjects and other links which are usually found in portals.

Today, it is a very fine line that separates subject directories and search engines. Most subject directories have added search engines to query their databases, while search engines are acquiring directories or creating their own.

What are the pros and cons of subject directories?

Directory editors usually organise directories which are arranged into subject categories and sub-categories. When you are clicking through several subjects to get to an actual world wide web page,

Subject Directories

this kind of organisation may appear long winded and boring, but this is also the strength of the subject directory. Because of the human oversight in subject directories, they usually deliver a higher quality of content and fewer results which are made out of context than search engines. Unlike search engines, most subject directories do not databases of their own. Instead of storing pages, they point to them. This situation sometimes creates problems for the user because, once accepted for inclusion in a directory, the World wide web page could change content and the editors might not realise it. The directory might continue to point to a page that has been moved or that no longer exists. Dead links are one of the real problems for subject directories, as is a perceived bias toward e-commerce sites.

When do you use subject directories?

Subject directories are best for browsing in general and for searches of a very general nature. They are very good sources for information on popular topics, organisations, commercial sites and products, but not so good with specifics. When you'd like to see what kind of information is available on the world wide web in a particular field or area of interest, simply go to a directory and browse through the subject categories.

CHAPTER 6
Other Databases

What are library gateways and specialised databases?

Library gateways are collections of databases and informational sites which are arranged by subject and have been, reviewed and recommended by specialists, usually librarians.

These gateway collections support the needs of research and reference by identifying and pointing to high quality pages on the world wide web. Specialised databases however are databases which have been created by professors, researchers, experts, governmental agencies, business interests, and other subject specialists and/or individuals who have a deep interest in, and more importantly a professional knowledge of, a particular field and have accumulated information and data about it.

What is the 'Invisible World Wide Web'?

There is a huge section of the world wide web that search engines cannot, or may not, index. It has been renamed the "Invisible World wide web" and it includes, among other things, pass-protected sites, documents behind firewalls, pdf files, archived material, interactive tools such as calculators and dictionaries, and the contents of databases. In other words, the invisible web is the part of the web which normal users are not able to access for various reasons. World wide web profilers agree that the Invisible World wide web, which is made up of thousands of such documents and databases, accounts for 60 to 80 percent of existing world wide web material. This is information you probably assumed you could access by using standard search engines, but that's not always the case. These resources are not usually visible to search engine spiders because they are embedded within individual world wide web sites.

Library gateways and speciality search tools are good sources to allow you to link directly to database information stored on the Invisible World wide web.

When do you use Library Gateways?

You should use library gateways when you are looking for high quality information sites on the

Other Databases

World wide web. You can be fairly certain that these sites have been reviewed and evaluated by subject specialists.

Library gateways and speciality search tools are very useful when you are looking for "subject-speciality" databases on the Invisible World wide web, e.g., news links, multimedia files, archives, mailing lists, people, job finders, and thousands of databases devoted to specific topics of interest. More and more of the more common search engines and subject directories are pointing to these subject-speciality databases as well, using direct links on their home pages. However, it is often easier to find the pages you seek by using a library gateway.

How do I evaluate World Wide Web pages?

Firstly, check the source.

You can expect to find anything and everything on the world wide web from silly sites, hoaxes, frivolous and serious personal pages, commercials, reviews, articles, full-text documents to academic courses, scholarly papers, reference sources, and scientific reports. This section will help you to work out which pages are reliable and which are not. You can tell a lot about the authenticity of a page by finding out all you can about its author or editor.

To be able to analyse this, you will need to know

how to read a world wide web address, or URL (Universal Resource Locator). Although this has been covered in detail, it is worth reminding yourself how to do this at this stage. Here's how to break down the URL: **http://www.bbc.co.uk/news/sport** and this is what it means -
- "http" is the transfer protocol (type of information being transferred)
- "www" is the host computer name (server name)
- "bbc" is the second-level domain name
- "news" is the directory name
- "sport" is the sub-directory name
- ".co.uk" shows it is based in the UK

Only a few top-level domains are currently recognised, but this is changing. Here is a list of the domains generally accepted by all:
- .co.uk – a site based in the UK
- .edu – educational site (usually a university or college)
- .com – commercial business site
- .gov – US governmental/non-military site (not in the UK)
- .net – networks, Internet service providers, organisations
- .org – US non-profit organisations and others (not in the UK)

Other Databases

In mid November 2000, the Internet Corporation for Assigned Names and Numbers (ICANN) voted to accept an additional seven new suffixes, which are expected to be made available to users by the middle or the end of 2001:

- .aero – will be restricted use by air transportation industry
- .biz – will be used by businesses
- .coop – restricted use by co-operatives
- .info – general use by both commercial and non-commercial sites
- .museum – restricted use by museums
- .name – general use by individuals
- .pro – restricted use by certified professionals and professional entities

It is worth noting at this stage that US is not generally used at the end of URL addresses because the Internet originated in the States, so the country suffixes were not needed until other countries joined in with the Net. It is, however, used to designate state and local government hosts, including many public schools in the US. Other countries have their own two letter codes as the final part of their domain names, e.g. .ca for Canada; .fr for France, etc..

The next thing you should consider when trying to work out the credibility of a web site is who is responsible for the page you are accessing. If it is a governmental agency or other official source, a university, a business, corporation or other commercial interest, there is a very fair chance that the page is fairly reliable as it will have been checked by a governing body and/or professionals to make sure that all the information contained in it is correct and factual. If, however, it was written and edited by an individual, you can generally presume that it is not necessarily so reliable. This is not necessarily the case, as the individual may have thoroughly researched the subject before writing the page, but it is fair to at least assume that there is no governing body checking the information that it contains. As a rule of thumb, you can usually rely on the .gov and .edu host names to present accurate information to you. The .net, .co.uk and .com are more uncertain and might require additional verification, as anyone can design their own site with these suffixes.

Next, you should make sure that you check the vital information. A reputable and reliable world wide web page will usually provide you with the following information;

The date or time in which it was last updated.

There is usually a mail-to link for questions, comments.

The name, address, telephone number, and e-mail address of page owner.

Finally, ask yourself if the page owner is not

Other Databases

readily recognisable, does he provide you with credentials or some information on his sources or authority? If none of the above are present, I would leave well alone.

Checking the content of a web page

On the world wide web, each individual can be his or her own publisher, and indeed many are. Do not accept everything you read just because it is printed on a world wide web page. Unlike educational books and news articles, world wide web sites are seldom reviewed or refereed by any governing bodies or professionals. It is therefore up to you to check for any prejudices and to determine their objectivity. It is worth looking to see of the site has a sponsor of any kind. If it does, there is a great likelihood that the page will represent and reflect the views and leanings of the sponsor. Similarly, any links that appear on the page may only appear there because they feel that page supports their views. Look to see if the page owner tells you when the page was last updated. If the information is not really current, it may not be of any use, depending on the subject you are researching. If you find the same information on another site, it may therefore be reliable.

Another tip is to try to distinguish between promotion, advertising, and serious content. This, admittedly, is getting to be more and more difficult, as an increasing number of pages must look to commercial support for their continuance.

How can I assess World Wide Web page stability?
There is no way to freeze a world wide web page in time. Unlike books which have publication dates, editions, ISBN numbers, etc.., world wide web pages are constantly being updated and altered. There is no governmental control on the world wide web. The page you quote from today might be changed or revised before you look at it again tomorrow, or it might disappear completely. The page owner might or might not mention the changes and, if the page is moved to a different web address, might or might not leave a forwarding address. You should always try to assess the stability of the pages you reference. Again, one of the best ways to do this is to look closely at the page sponsor, last dated updated, and the authority of the author.

A top tip to remember when you are writing a paper and using world wide web pages as source material, you should always keep a back-up of what you find on the world wide web, either as a printout or saved to a disk, so that you can prove and reuse your sources later on if you have to.

CHAPTER 7
Meta Search Engines

What are Meta Search Engines?
Meta search engines do not crawl the world wide web compiling their own searchable databases like a conventional search engine. Instead, they search the databases of many sets of individual search engines at the same time, from a single site and using the same interface. Meta searchers provide a quick way of finding out which engines are retrieving the best results for you in your search. In other words, meta search engines will search the indexes of many search engines, rather than searching the web.

How do Meta search display their results?
Meta search engines present the results of their searches in two ways. The first is as a Single List. Most meta searchers display multiple-engine search results in a single merged list, and there is also the

advantage that any duplicates have been removed by this stage. Secondly, there are Multiple Lists. Some meta searchers do not collect and compare multiple-engine search results, but display them instead in separate lists as they are received from each engine. Duplicate entries may therefore appear and waste your time.

What are the pros and cons of meta searchers?

One disadvantage of meta search engines is they don't offer the huge choice of search options that individual search engines do. When you begin a key word or phrase search on a meta search engine, you are usually unable to control the search as far as how the search is conducted. Although meta search engines query a number of individual search engines, few query all of the major search engines another problem is that meta search engines do not return every one of the results that they have retrieved from the individual engines they search. However, the searches they do return are always taken from the top of each search engine list, and therefore they tend to be much more relevant. The main advantage of a meta searcher is that it is extremely fast.

Meta Search Engines

When do you use meta search engines?
You should use meta searchers when you are in a hurry. They are useful in obtaining a quick overview on a subject and/or a unique term but they won't retrieve very detailed results. You should use meta searchers when you are carrying out a fairly simple search and also when you are not having any luck finding documents with a normal search engine.

Tips for searching the World Wide Web...
To begin with, it is best to realise that the more carefully you think about the key words you are using to allow your search engine to find information for you. In other words, it's always a good idea to *think* about your search before you begin.

You should have a basic search strategy in your head, but don't take too long, by asking yourself what it is you want to find. Do you want to find a specific piece of information about something? Or do you want to find out more about a particular subject? Or do you simply want to browse your way through the world wide web? The way in which you answer these questions will help you to decide the way you will find the information you require. If you want to find out a specific piece of information, for example, you wish to find out all about the Live Aid event, you would simply type into your search engine "Live

Aid". This may bring up a few possible world wide web sites which contain these words, but it should also bring up a link to give you further information on the concert that was held.

If however, you wish to find out more about a subject that you are interested in, such as US History, you would type that into your search engine. Again, your search engine will more than likely bring up possibilities that are of little use to you, but you should be able to find something that is useful to you from the search you have made. Lastly, if you wish to simply browse the world wide web, you can just start by typing in a word or two that you feel may be interesting, such as today's news. This will bring up a whole list of possibilities which will then give you link after link to other world wide web pages and sites. It is also worthwhile to think about carrying out the same search using different search engines, as each one searches in a slightly different way and looks for different key words, so may bring you completely different possible links from all the others. It is also worth noting at this point that you may try the sites of encyclopaedias for US History and also newspapers, TV world wide web sites etc. etc., as they may have further information which, in turn, gives you possible key words to use in your next search.

When you begin to conduct a search, it is best to

Meta Search Engines

bear in mind that the best results will be those that are generally made up of nouns, for example, Glasgow shopping, as opposed to Where can I shop in Glasgow. This keeps the wording to a minimum, but the main words are used – Glasgow and shopping. Another help when you are searching, is to make sure that you always keep the main and most important word at the beginning of your words. That is to say that "Glasgow" is more important than "shopping" as it is specifically Glasgow that is required. If you used the word shopping first, you would have lists of shopping centres everywhere, not just in the UK!

A useful point that is not well used in searing the world wide web, is that if you place a + sign in front of each noun, they will all be searched and only links that have all the matching words will be offered to you. This means that *only* information about shops in Glasgow would be offered to you if you type "+Glasgow +shopping", rather than general information about Glasgow and tourism etc..

It is a good idea to try to avoid very common or overused words in your search, such as hot or blue, as they will bring up too many possible links which are of little or no use to the search you are carrying out. Only use such words if they are part of the phrase or subject, such as hot chocolate. Conversely, it is a good idea to think about words which may be used throughout the page you are searching for, as this will provide you with a closer link to them. An example of this could be if you are looking for information about the pop group Queen, if you simply typed in "Queen" you would be offered links from Queen Elizabeth II to Queens throughout history. So, in this case, it is fairly obvious that the name Freddie Mercury will be used at some point in any of the world wide web sites, so your key words in your search may be "+Queen +Freddie +Mercury" and this should give you some success. If in this case, you did not know the names of any of the group, you could simply type in a title of a popular song by them, such as *Bohemian Rhapsody*.

Basic search tips summarised

Use the plus + and minus - signs in front of words to force them to be included and/or excluded in searches. Remember there should be no space between the sign and the key word you are using.

For example, +anorexia -bulimia, would give you information on anorexia, but would exclude pages that were on bulimia, as some search engines would bring up both of them, whichever one was being searched for.

Use double quotation marks " " around phrases to ensure that they are searched exactly as is, with the

Meta Search Engines

words side by side in the same order.

For example, "Bye bye Miss American Pie" would bring you information on the title of that song, rather than just telling you about any page which has these key words present.

Put your most important key words first in the search you are carrying out

for example, +elephant +African, would give you only information on African elephants, but the "elephant" part of the phrase is more important to narrow down your search.

Type key words and phrases in lower case to find both lower and upper case versions. Typing capital letters will usually return only an exact match.

For example, the word "president" will retrieve both president and President

Use truncation and wild cards (e.g., *) to look for variations in spelling and word form.

For example, librar* would return matches for returns library, libraries, librarian, etc..

Combine phrases with key words, using the double quotes and the plus + and/or minus -signs.

For example, +"lung cancer" +bronchitis -smoking

In this case, if you use a key word with a +sign, you must put the +sign in front of the phrase as well. When searching for a phrase alone, the +sign is not necessary.

When searching a document on the world wide web site for your key words, use the "find" command on that page. (usually obtained by pressing Ctrl+F or by clicking on the "edit" on the toolbar at the top).

Know the default settings your search engine uses (OR or AND). This will have an effect on how you configure your search statement because, if you don't use any signs (+, -, " "), the engine will default to its own settings.

CHAPTER 8
Using Boolean Searches

What is a Boolean?!
Boolean logic takes its name from a British mathematician called George Boole, who lived from 1815–1864, who wrote about a system of logic designed to produce better search results by formulating precise queries. He called it the "calculus of thought", and it is today known as a Boolean Search. From his writings, we have derived Boolean logic and its operators – AND, OR, and NOT, which we use to link words and phrases for more precise queries on the Internet. This method is also used in libraries, so you may have encountered this before. The following section will only describe the method and purpose it has for searching the Internet.

The word AND
The Boolean use of the word AND will narrow your

search by retrieving only documents that contain every single one of the key words you enter. The more words you enter, the narrower your search will become.

For example, truth AND justice
or
truth AND justice AND ethics AND congress

The word OR
The Boolean use of the word OR will help to expand your search. This is done by returning documents in which either or both key words appear. Since the OR operator is usually used for key words that are similar or for synonymous, the more key words you enter, the more documents you will be able to (hopefully) retrieve.

For example, Westlife OR Boyzone
or
Westlife OR Boyzone OR Five OR A1

Use of the word NOT
The Boolean use of the word NOT or AND NOT will help you to limit your search by returning only your first key word but not the second, even if the first word appears in that document, too.

A good example of this is bulimia AND NOT

Using Boolean Searches

anorexia, as they are similar illnesses, so many search engines will be programmed to bring up links with either word used, even if the word does not form part of the search.

What is NESTING?

Nesting is the term used in Boolean searches for using parentheses or brackets ( ). It is an extremely effective way to combine several search statements into one search statement. The brackets should be used to separate key words when you are using more than one operator and three or more key words.

For example, (scotch OR bourbon) AND NOT (beer OR wine)

For the best results, always enclose OR statements in brackets.

Implied Boolean Operators

Implied Boolean operators use the plus + and minus - symbols in place of the full Boolean operators, AND and NOT. Typing a + or - sign in front of a word will force the inclusion or exclusion of that word in the search statement.

For example, +bulimia -anorexia

Similarly, putting double quotation marks " " around two or more words will force them to be searched as a phrase in that exact order.

For example, "green tea". If the wording was not enclosed in quotes, the words would be searched randomly, and would not usually appear in that order. While full Boolean operators are usually accepted only in the advanced search option of search engines, implied Boolean operators are accepted in the basic search options of nearly every search engines.

Defaults regarding Boolean searches
Boolean logic is not always simple or easy. Different search engines handle Boolean operators differently. For example, some will accept NOT, others will accept ANDNOT as one word, others AND NOT as two words. Some will require the operators to be typed in capital letters while others do not.

Some search engines use drop-down menu options to spell out the Boolean logic in short phrases. For example, "All of the words" or "Must contain" equates to AND; "Any of the words" or "Should contain" equates to OR; and "Must not contain" equates to NOT. This will make it easier for you to use the Boolean language that is acceptable by your search engine.

In your search statement, if you enter more than one key word without using any symbol, whether it

Using Boolean Searches

is with a full or implied Boolean operator, the search engine will automatically default to either the Boolean AND or the Boolean OR. This could radically alter your search. It is therefore very important that you find out what the defaults of the search engine you are using and how your search engine handles Boolean operators or your search results may not be what you expected.

Strange things can happen for other reasons as well. Sometimes the relevance ranking systems that search engines use can throw off your search by ignoring some of the words in your search statement. This might happen when the search engine recognises your string of separate key words as a phrase in its list of predetermined phrases or when it is responding to its own internal list of "stop words" (explained next!). Whatever the case, you may never know the real reason why your search retrieves so many irrelevant responses.

Stop words

Stop words are, confusingly, words that many search engines DON'T stop for when searching texts and titles on the world wide web. In fact, in order to cut down on response times, these engines will routinely ignore stop words. To explain it more simply, a stop word is really a small and common words, such as parts of speech (adverbs, conjunctions, prepositions, or forms of "to be"). Examples include a, an, and, as, at, be, if, into, it, of, on, or, the, to, with, etc.. Not all search engines recognise the same stop words. In addition, their lists can and do change frequently. If you begin a search at a site that maintains a list of stop words and you type any of those words into your search statement – even in phrases surrounded by quotes – they will be ignored.

What are proximity operators in Boolean searching?

Proximity, or positional, operators (NEAR, ADJ, SAME, FBY) are not really part of Boolean logic, but they serve a similar function in formulating search statements. Not all search engines accept proximity operators, but a few accept NEAR in their advanced search option. The NEAR operator allows you to search for terms situated within a specified distance of each other in any order. The closer they are, the higher the document appears in the results list. Using NEAR, when possible, in place of the Boolean AND usually returns more relevant results. Even fewer search engines accept ADJ (adjacent to). ADJ works as a phrase except that the two terms, which must appear adjacent to each other in the world wide web page, can appear in any order.

For example, Ernest ADJ Hemingway returns both Ernest Hemingway and Hemingway Ernest. Other proximity operators, such as SAME – key words found in the same field – and FBY – followed by – are used as advanced searching techniques in library and other specialised databases that contain bibliographic references or references to journal articles.

Tips for Boolean searches summarised

In Boolean searches, always enclose OR statements in parentheses.

For example, "financial aid" AND (bank OR loans)

Always use CAPS when typing Boolean operators in your search statements. Most engines require that the operators (AND, OR, AND NOT/NOT) be capitalised. The engines that don't will accept either CAPS or lower case, so you'll always be safe if you stick to CAPS.

For example, "eating disorder" AND (bulimia OR anorexia)

Chapter 9
On the Internet

What is a Home Page?

A home page on the world wide web can have two very different and distinct meanings. The first definition of a home page is the page that is present when you open up your world wide web browser. This is your "home base" for exploring the world wide web. It is usually the page displaying your ISP. If you find that you have got lost while you have been exploring various links on the world wide web, you can simply click on the "home" icon and that will allow you to be taken right back to your home base.

The second meaning that can be taken from the term home page is the first page or the open door into the published documents of something you are looking at on the world wide web. To put this in a more simple way, it is the first page that you will be taken to when you enter a world wide web site. The home page of a world wide web site will give you access to every page that is connected to that Internet site by following links to each area of the site from the home page.

Official and Unofficial World Wide Web sites

Sites can be official or unofficial. Official sites are those which have been set up to represent a company or charity or pop group, for instance, BY that company or pop group. That is to say that a world wide web site for Childline would be set up by Childline and would be for the use of people wishing to find out more about the charity or to make a donation etc.. This would be an official site for the charity. Unofficial sites are more often made by fans or collectors or people who are simply interested enough in a subject to have the desire to share that information with others who may also wish to learn about it. The most common unofficial sites are those dedicated to famous people such as pop stars or film stars. The world wide web sites have not been created and set up by the pop group or their management company, and has not been done with their permission, but has been created by a fan to give facts, pictures and information to others about their idols.

On the Internet

World Wide Web addresses themselves

World wide web addresses are also known as URLs or Uniform Resource Locators. Every world wide web page has a unique URL which identifies it from all others, with three different, distinct parts. The URL always begins with what is known as the Protocol (in other words http:// or ftp://). The protocol breaks down into the host name and the file path. The host name is everything which is typed before the first /, and the file path is everything after and including the first /. It is not important for a complete beginner to know this, but it is worth explaining out of interest. An example of this is http://www.bbc.co.uk/news/. The first part of the URL - http – tells us that it is a hyper text file which is on the world wide web. The domain name – www.bbc.co.uk – tells us that it is a site which is based in the United Kingdom, and the file within the BBC world wide web site that is being located is /news/.

What is downloading?

When you are on the Internet, there will be many opportunities as you browse through all the pages to download a file. The basic definition of downloading is to retrieve a file from a host computer. In other words, it is possible to download a file, a music or video clip, software for your PC etc. etc.. it is as easy as a click of your mouse to actually download information, but to do this, you will need to have a program that is able to handle file transfer protocol, or FTP. There are a couple of methods you can use for this. You can either use your world wide web browser to download files, or you can install a separate program which is used simply for downloading. Using your world wide web browser is by far the easiest and cheapest way to download, but stand-alone browsers are generally more advanced and have more features for you to use. This is only really necessary if you are downloading vast amounts of information, or if you find that you download regularly.

Many companies and Internet programmers offer Internet users the chance to download software free of charge. It is well worth reading any small print, as some companies may SAY it is free, but you are only actually given very little information that is free. When you get to a certain point, you may have to pay up. It is wise to be cautious, but do not become too suspicious, as many companies do indeed offer completely free information that you can download, or they will give you a taster of what you can buy from them by downloading their programs. Other companies simply ask you to agree to pay after you have reached a certain period, whether it is after a certain time period or after a certain amount of

On the Internet

information has been given for free. If you do have to pay at some point, this is usually pointed out at the earliest stage, so there shouldn't be any nasty surprises later on down the line.

How do I download?

If you are using Netscape or Internet Explorer as your world wide web browser, they are both capable of downloading any information you may find on the Net. It is very simple to physically download the information you require. All you do is simply point your cursor at the link and click your mouse on it. The file will begin to download, and the company that is supplying it may ask for your name or an e-mail address just for their records. The downloading process will usually take a few minutes, but not much longer than that. It is worth noting that you should be able to use the Internet while the program is being downloaded. Downloading information is generally different each time, but there will always be prompts and instructions explaining what to type in or what to click on for the download to be complete. Often, information you wish to have is made up of many different programs. The companies and programmers have made it easier and quicker for you to download these programs by compressing all of the files into one larger file. This is a great solution, but in many cases you will need a special program to uncompress that file, then giving you access to the programs contained within it.

What is a virus?

One term that has been used time and time again for many years is the term computer virus. It is a term that most of us will be familiar with, as the term is used regularly on the news and by the general public. It is safe to say that a virus is something that no one wants on their PC system. If you wish to download, or regularly download files and information, you are risking infection by a virus. A virus can be defined as a program that will infect various areas of your PC and Internet, and it can spread from your PC to another PC, through the use of e-mail, for instance. A virus can infect your computer if you open an infected program, or if you use an infected disk in your PC. There are viruses that will not do much damage to any of your equipment, but there are others that are much more serious and can destroy everything that you have saved on your hard drive. Another type of virus that can spread is known as a worm. It's purpose is to spread to other PCs, but you do not even need to do anything for this to happen. They will simply spread by clinging onto something you have on your PC,

On the Internet

such as your e-mail address book, and will send itself to each and every person that is present there. This means that worms can spread at an alarming rate – much faster than a program virus itself. The third type of virus than can appear is known as a Trojan. This type will do something that you are not expecting it to, or will do something without you knowing about it until a later stage. The purpose of a Trojan is not to spread, like the other two types of virus, but it is usually there to allow a hacker into your computer while you are working online.

The best way to avoid and stop viruses attacking your system is by ensuring that you have security devices in place on your PC, such as a virus scanner, which is a necessity if you are downloading. The latest versions of any software will allow you to keep a virus scanner running in the memory of your computer for the duration that the computer is on. This will alert you if it detects any virus behaviour on your system and will stop it before it can harm anything. It will also combine with your file decompressor to allow you to scan each and every file that you download before you even consider installing it onto your computer.

What is a server?
A server is really the piece of computer hardware that

carries out all the work when you are using the Internet. These servers work all night and all day and are connected up to lots and lots of cables that pass information back and forth. People that request information from these machines are called clients – that's the computer that you are using. If is wasn't for these servers, we would not be able to get any information from the Net and we would be unable to send and receive e-mails. All of these servers and clients talk to each other through a variety of different languages which are known as protocols. For example, the part of many world wide web sites that you will see – http:// – stands for hypertext transfer protocol, which is how the World wide web works. There are other protocols for electronic mail, simple computer file transfers and many more. Computer information is sent from computer to computer using numerical addresses called IP addresses. The IP address tells each computer where the file came from or where it needs to go. An IP address is a series of four numbers connected by dots. For example, 204.107.252.1.

To make it easy for users of the Internet, like you and me, to work out where things are going, most IP addresses also have a unique domain address attached to them. A domain name would be something like www.yell.com. The domain names are translated into IP addresses by servers called Domain

On the Internet

Name Servers. Each server not only has its own domain name, but can also host other domains as well. A domain that is hosted by another domain is basically a section of the host's memory and is called a virtual domain.

Clients can also request specific sections – called directories – of a domain. These sections are indicated by a forward slash or /. Clients can even request a specific file in that specific directory. The file name is usually the last piece of information after the slashes. The combination of the protocol – http:// – and the domain name and whatever directories and other information that comes after the domain name is called a uniform resource locator or URL. So when you type a URL into the location bar of your browser and hit the return key, the protocol part of the URL tells the servers on the Internet what kind of request you are sending, the domain part tells all the servers along the line where to route the request. When the domain receives the request, it interprets the rest of the URL, finds the file you asked for (or creates one) and sends it off to your IP address. Depending on how overworked the server is, how good your connection is, and how fast your computer is, you'll get the page. If it takes too long, chances are that the computer program you used will give up and ask you to check the address and try again.

What is an IRC?

You have probably heard of chat rooms which are used on the Internet as they are increasingly becoming a very popular part of the Internet. It is a term which is often used to describe any part of the Net where you can communicate with others, but there are in fact many ways to communicate. the first way is through an IRC. With IRC, or Internet Relay Chat, you can participate in live chat with others on the Internet. This is different to e-mail because you are answering and sending e-mails to each other, rather than it actually being a live way to communicate. it also gives you the opportunity to chat to more than one person at a time. If you wish to say something, everyone who is in the chat room at that time will receive your message at the same time. This means that there are people who you do not know, from all over the world, who you can begin to "chat to" online. This could be based on a shared interest, such as a pop group or a hobby, or it could simply be a chat room where the aim is to make and meet new friends. You simply select a chat room that you wish to use from a list of thousands that are divided up by their subject. There is a topic about almost every subject that you could ever think of, but if you don't see one that you like, you could even create your own! The chat rooms on the Internet are usually for informal, social purposes

On the Internet

rather than for business use. A chat room will allow you to see just how vast and how accessible the Internet is for everyone all over the world. It an be a strange experience, talking to people from various parts of the world at the same time, when you have never seen them or met them before. Chat rooms are becoming an increasingly popular way to meet new people physically. In other words, you may spend a while in a chat room and realise that you have a lot in common with a certain individual you talk to regularly. This can often lead to an exclusive friendship that then begin to become an e-mail friendship where only these two individuals are messaging each other. It may then lead to the individuals meeting face to face as they feel they have struck up a good relationship with them. It is advisable to treat such meetings with caution because, remember, they could have told you any lies about themselves as you have not actually met before. They could be a completely different age than they have suggested, as they felt that they could be who they wanted to behind the shield of their PC. Just remember that you don't know them as well as you would know someone you met at work or in a pub, for instance.

Many companies, such as AOL or, in the UK, the BBC, have live chats with celebrities, such as pop stars and film stars. They will be heavily advertised and all you will have to do to take part is join the specific group to be able to join in with the live interview. If you use Windows, the most popular IRC program to use for chatting is mIRC. They are fairly easy to use. All you really have to do to begin is choose a name for yourself that you will be known as every time you enter the IRC, and secondly you have to enter your name and e-mail address to register. Always remember that you probably want to remain anonymous, so it is usually the best option to choose a different name so that you won't be "found out" by anyone who may also be in the chat room at the time. this is very possible to happen, especially if you are chatting in a room dedicated to an interest that you an a friend have a passion about. There is a very real chance of them being in the room at the same time. this may not be something that concerns you but remember that you may say things about people you know that you do not expect to be chatting too! One of the disadvantages of IRC is that the second you join the chat, the rest of the people in the room will be told that you are there, and your alias will be there as long as you stay in the chat room. In other words, you can't really just join the chat room and not say anything, because all the other users will know you are there! It is possible to find out some very basic information about the others who are in the room, by right-clicking your mouse on their name on the list. The information will only be what you have inputted, but others may check out who you are too – so be careful what you tell them! The problem that many people encounter when they first use an IRC is that there is a whole new language used in them. People will use abbreviations and code words and new users may not understand, but if you genuinely want to get into this way of chatting, stick with it and you will soon pick it up and join in. the other disadvantage of an IRC is that you will in fact need to use a separate browser to use them.

What is a news group?

News groups and chat rooms however, only need you to have a world wide web browser which, obviously, you will have if you are using the Net at all. News groups are a part of the Internet that will allow you to read and respond to messages posted by other members of the Internet. Like IRC, news groups are listed and divided up by topic. There are currently around 20,000 news groups in existence on the Net, so the chances are that you will find at least quite a few that you would like to be a part of. There is most likely an option in your News Reader that will allow you to list all of the news groups, so you can scroll through and choose which ones you would like to subscribe to, or it will allow you to just enter the address of the news group you want to check out. After you have subscribed to your favourite news groups your news reader will automatically load the new messages from those news groups every time you load it. News groups are great for people who like to stay up to date on a particular topic. They are also a good place to go if you have a question about a topic and you cannot find it elsewhere on the Internet, because you can simply post a message and most likely you will get a few responses quickly from other Internet users.

Book marking/favourites

It is inevitable that at some time during your many searches on the Net, that you will find sites or pages that you may wish to return to at a later time. This may be that there is too much for you to read at that point, or that the site will be useful to your work or a hobby, or it might be a shopping page that you feel you will use regularly. If you find a world wide web site that you would like to return to in the future, you can add it to your "favourites". In other words, the page or site that you are currently at can be saved in your own personal folder for use at a later date. This allows you to go back to the page or site without having to take time to write down the world wide web address to keep and then taking the time

On the Internet

to type the address manually when you wish to go to the site again. Some systems call this process "book marking" but they work in the same way, whether they are favourites or bookmarks. It is a very easy process to carry out. When you are at a page or site that you wish to add to your favourites folder, simply click the cursor on "favourites", which is on the toolbar at the top of the screen, and then click the cursor on "add to favourites". A pop up will give you the option to change the name of the saved site. This is very worthwhile. Imagine you have 10 sites saved which are all on the same topic – it is a good idea to call the site a word or phrase that will remind you what it contains that is slightly different from the other sites and pages you have saved. For instance, if you have a few sites saved under favourites which are all about cars, you could call one site "Ferrari", another one could be "Formula 1" and another could be "market prices of cars", just to differentiate the differences between each site.

What is screen capturing and logging?

From time to time, you will see messages on the Net that you want to save for later viewing – whether it is a recipe, a news article, something you want to learn more about or something you've never heard of. This is where screen capturing and logging come in to play. When you tell your communications software to capture a screen, it will open a file in your computer (usually in the same directory or folder used by the software) and will capture or "dump" an image of whatever happens to be on your screen at the time. Logging works a bit differently. When you issue a logging command, you tell the software to open a file (again, usually in the same directory or folder as used by the software) and then give it a name. Then, until you turn off the logging command, everything that scrolls on your screen is copied into that file, sort of like recording on videotape. This is useful for capturing long documents that scroll for several pages. If you were using screen capture to carry this out, you would have to repeat the same command for each new screen. Terminal emulation is a way for your computer to copy, or emulate, the way other computers put information on the screen and accept commands from a keyboard. In general, most systems on the Net use a system called VT100. Fortunately, almost all communications programs now on the market support this system as well, so you should make sure yours does.

What Protocol should I use?
A protocol is a way for two networks to talk to each other. There are two basic settings of protocols. In

On the Internet

general, UNIX-based systems use 7-1-E protocols, while MS-DOS-based systems use 8-1-N. What if you don't know what kind of system you're connecting to? Try one of the settings. If you get what looks like gobbledegook when you connect, you may need the other setting. If so, you can either change the setting while connected, and then hit enter, or hang up and try again with the other setting. It's also possible your modem and the modem at the other end can't agree on the right BPS rate. If changing the protocols doesn't work, try using another BPS rate (but no faster than the one listed for your modem). Don't worry, remember, you can't break anything by simply pressing some buttons. If something looks wrong, it probably is wrong. Change your settings and try again. You won't learn much without trial, error and effort.

The Clinton administration, arguably the first led by people who know how to use not only computer networks but computers, pushed for the creation of a series of "information superhighways". Right now, we are in the network equivalent of the early 1950s, just before the creation of a massive highway network. There are plenty of educational and interesting things out there, but you have to wander along two-lane roads, and have a good map, to get to them effectively. The Net remains a somewhat complicated and mysterious place. To get something out of the

Net today, you have to spend a fair amount of time with a Net expert or with a book or manual. If you compare this with the telephone, which now also provides access to large amounts of information through the push of a button, or a computer network such as Prodigy, which one navigates through simple commands and mouse clicks.

Internet system administrators have begun to realise that not all people want to learn the complicated world of UNIX, and that that fact does not make them bad people! We are already seeing the development of simple interfaces that will put the Net's power to use by millions of people. You can already see their influence in the menus of ISPs and the world wide web, which require no complex computing skills but which open the gates to thousands of information resources. Mail programs and text editors promise much of the power of older programs such as emacs at a fraction of the complexity. Some software engineers are looking at taking this even further, by creating graphic interfaces that will let somebody navigate the Internet just by clicking on the screen with a mouse or by calling up an easy text editor, sort of the way one can now navigate a Macintosh computer.

How advanced is the net?

For every database now available through the Internet, there are probably three or four that are not. Government agencies are only slowly beginning to connect their pages and pages of information to the Net. Several commercial sales companies, from database services to booksellers, have made their services available through the Net. Few people now use one of the Net's more interesting applications. A standard known as MIME lets you send audio and graphics files in a message. Eventually, this standard could allow for distribution of even small video displays over the Net. All of this will require vast new amounts of Net power, to handle both the millions of new people who will jump onto the Net and the new applications they want. Replicating a moving image on a computer screen alone takes a phenomenal amount of computer bits, and computing power to arrange them. All of this combines into a National Information Infrastructure able to move billions of bits of information in one second – the kind of power needed to hook information into every business and house. As these superhighways grow, so will the ways to access them – a high-speed road does you little good if you can't get to it. The costs of modems seem to fall as fast as those of computers. High-speed modems are becoming increasingly affordable. With a higher speed modem, you can download a satellite weather image of Aberdeen in less than two minutes, a file that, with a slower modem could take up to 20 minutes to download. Eventually, homes could be connected directly to a national digital network. Most long-distance phone traffic is already carried in digital form, through high-volume optical fibres. Phone companies are very slowly working to extend these fibres so they make the last step to the home. The Electronic Frontier Foundation in the US is working to ensure these links are affordable. Beyond the technical questions are increasingly difficult social, political and economic issues. Who will be able to have access to these services, and at what cost? If we live in an information age, are we laying the seeds for a new information under-class, who are unable to compete with those fortunate enough to have the money and skills needed to manipulate new communications channels? Who, in fact, will decide who has access to what? As more companies realise the potential profits which can be made in the new information infrastructure, what happens to such systems as Usenet, possibly the world's first successful anarchistic system, where everybody can say whatever they want? When boundaries lose their meaning in cyberspace, the question might even be who is the law? What if a practice that is legal in one country is committed in another country where it is

On the Internet

illegal, over a computer network that crosses through a third country?

What happens when things go wrong?

As the Internet grows more and more popular, its resources come under much more of a strain. For instance, if you try to use AOL in the middle of the day on the East Coast of the US, you'll sometimes notice that it will take a very long time for a particular menu or database search to come up. Sometimes, you'll even get a message that there are too many people connected to whichever service you're trying to use and so you can't get in. The only real alternative is to either try again in 20 minutes or so, or wait until later in the day, when the load might be lower. Certain MS-DOS communications programs have stupidly long names or addresses. If it is not copied accurately, there will be problems connecting to that page. The best was to rectify it is to save it to your favourites folder and then change the name of it. If that name is longer than one line, you won't be able to backspace all the way back to the first line if you want to give it a simpler name. Backspace as far as you can. Then, when you get ready to download it to your home computer, remember that the file name will be truncated on your end, because of MS-DOS's file-naming limitations. BUT this may actually cause another problem – it may be that your computer rejects the whole thing. What should you do if this happens? Instead of saving it to your favourites file, you should actually e-mail it to yourself. It should show up in your mail by the time you go off-line. Then, open your e-mail to yourself and then use your e-mail command for saving it to your favourites file. You will now be able to name it anything you want and subsequently you can now download it. It may seem a very long way to go about this, but at least it will work for you.

CHAPTER 10
What is E-mail?

E-mail – what is it and how do I use it?

E-mail is the term used to describe the sending and receiving of messages from somebody else who is online. The sending of e-mail, or electronic mail, has become one of the most commonly used forms of the Internet. It has given its users a new way of communicating which combines the immediacy of a phone call and the opportunity for considered reflection possible in a letter. E-mail makes it possible for students to stay in touch with their peers and with the teaching staff where a busy timetable may make this otherwise difficult. In other words, electronic mail, or e-mail as it is known today, is a way of sending a letter or a message or even a document from your Microsoft files or from the Internet to someone. Both people must have an e-mail address to be able to do this, but it is so easy to set up an e-mail account that this is not a problem in today's e-mail age. Most e-mail accounts are even free of charge, as they are part of your Internet service provider's service to you, the customer. Every day, the users of the Internet send each other literally billions of e-mail messages. If you are online for a lot of the time, you yourself may send a dozen or two e-mails each day without even thinking about it. Obviously, e-mail has become an extremely popular communication tool in a very short time.

Netscape Communicator and Microsoft Internet Explorer allow you to read and send e-mail as well as surf the World wide web. You can also use MIME (Multipurpose Internet Mail Extensions) to send files attached to your emails, whether it consists of text, pictures, or programs. If you have used a computer to type a letter, then you have most of the skills needed to send e-mail. The only difference is that with the usual methods of sending mail, you would have to print out the letter and put it in a mailbox, but with e-mail you press a key or two and the letter is transmitted electronically to the e-mailbox of the recipient, who can typically read your letter within a few seconds.

What exactly is an e-mail message?

The very first e-mail message was sent in 1971 by an engineer named Ray Tomlinson. Prior to this, you

What is E-mail?

could only send messages to users on a single machine, that is to say you could leave a message for another user who would be using the same PC at a later stage. Tomlinson's breakthrough was that he made it possible to send messages to other machines that were on the Internet, using the @ sign to show the receiving machine. An e-mail message has always been simply a message made up of text, or a piece of writing sent to an intended recipient. When you send an e-mail message to a friend, you are therefore sending a piece of text. In the beginning and even today, e-mail messages tended to be very short, brief pieces of text, although the ability to add attachments now makes many e-mail messages quite long. Even with attachments, however, e-mail messages continue to be text messages. This will be explained later.

E-mail is the Internet's most popular tool. Even if you never or rarely surf the World wide web, you will still probably end up using e-mail at some point. Whether it is for work or for social purposes, sending photos or receiving jokes, e-mail is an extremely useful and cheap form of communication – it is even cheaper than sending a letter or making a phonecall! But there is a lot to know if you wish to be able to use e-mail effectively, and even someone who has used e-mail for a while might not know all the tips and tricks of using e-mail software.

This section will help you through the different types of e-mail options that are available to you. It will also give you some tips as to how to use e-mail effectively and efficiently.

E-mail is the Internet's version of sending a letter or a piece of text. It is fast and very user-friendly tool to use and, as previously mentioned, is the most used part of the Internet. It is also a very good way to write a letter, as it is not important to have a set layout or font, and it can be set up so that all of your emails are signed off in the same way each time, without you having to manually type it. E-mails are immediate and allow the recipient to instantly reply to a mail within seconds. To use e-mail, you will need to have a means of sending and receiving them, so will need to have an e-mail account. You may have an e-mail program as part of the software which was supplied by your Internet Service Provider, such as Freeserve, AOL, or CompuServe, which supplies your Internet connection. If not, you may have an e-mail account as part of your world wide web browser, which would usually be Netscape and Internet Explorer). Alternatively you may prefer to use another piece of dedicated e-mail software which someone has recommended to you, such as Eudora or Quick Mail. If you have none of these, it is easy and quick to subscribe to e-mail through any of the ISPs and search engines. An added bonus of this is

What is E-mail?

that these accounts are usually free of charge.

Whichever method you use, they all work in a similar way, and will give you the facility to write, send, receive, store and manage your mail.

To send emails to friends and family, and to sign up for e-mail services, you will need to have your own e-mail address, which will look something like this;

jsmith@bbc.co.uk

- jsmith is the name of the user
- @ is read as 'at'
- bbc is the name which the BBC has registered with the Internet Society
- . is read as 'dot'
- co means the name belongs to a company
- uk means the name is on a computer in the United Kingdom

therefore, if you were asked to read out this e-mail address, you would read it as, "j dot smith at bbc dot co dot uk".

Every e-mail address has two parts which consist of a user name and a domain name.

A domain name usually includes the name of the organisation which owns the computer – bbc.co.uk is j.smith's domain. So the domain name often identifies the organisation who will manage your e-mail – "bbc.co.uk" or "hotmail.com" or "yahoo.com".

Sometimes a domain name will not only refer to a computer or organisation, but is simply a customised name which can be routed anywhere. The user name is your unique at that organisation. It doesn't matter what name you use, because whichever name you register under will be unique to you – there are no two e-mail addresses that are identical. It is a bit like a home address – there are no two addresses in the world that are exactly the same. Your user name may be your real name – j.smith - or a made up name, it simply doesn't matter as long as you know it and can tell other people what it is. If there are many people registered with the organisation who have the same user name, they will usually give you a number as well, so that the addresses are still different. For instance, you may have the address , or j.smith101@bbc.co.uk.

There are lots of ways to get an e-mail address. If you have an Internet account with one of the dial up services then they may offer you multiple e-mail addresses – BT Internet gives every account five addresses. They can set one of them up for you if you have difficulty in doing so.

Setting up your own account can cost anything from nothing at all, if you go with a free service – but always read the small print to watch out for hidden charges – to around £8 per month. When you open an account with an Internet Service

Provider you will be given an e-mail address and you can choose the first part yourself, from a selection, so it would be something like: myname@yahoo.com. The part which is before the @ is you, the section after is your ISP's 'domain', or the address of the computer that permanently keeps your mailbox. Some Internet service providers give you several mailboxes on an account and may let you rename part of the domain yourself, such as myname@myaccount.isp.net

Alternatively, or additionally you can use your Internet access to set up a free world wide web-based e-mail account with one of the many free world wide web-based services – these are slightly different from ordinary e-mail services, as they are accessed exclusively through the World wide web. When you open an account with an Internet Service Provider as well as your e-mail address, you should receive the special software to receive and compose e-mail with. This should give you an inbox and an outbox and a way of filing stuff you want to keep.

Free e-mail!

If you're planning on using your e-mail on another computer, for example if you wish to send or receive e-mail when you are travelling in another country or on holiday, some will let you read e-mail from any world wide web browser, and some let you send it using a world wide web browser as well – ask your Internet Service Provider what facilities they have for doing this. This is becoming more common to do this because when you access the World wide web in another country, say in an Internet cafe, you will not have your own e-mail software which you need to download your own mail – all you will have is a world wide web browser.

If you have an ISP which cannot offer world wide web access to your mail it's worth setting up another type of e-mail account – instead of or in addition to your ordinary account – a free world wide web-based e-mail account, such as Hotmail, Yahoo!, or Excite. All these services will let you send and receive messages wherever you can find a computer that is connected to the Net. You can send and receive world wide web e-mail by simply connecting to the service provider's world wide web site, with any browser anywhere in the world, and following the on screen instructions. This can also be useful if you want to view mail in several different locations which as college, work and the cybercafe.

Why do they provide free e-mail?
The providers usually make money by charging for advertising. There really isn't any catch with using

What is E-mail?

one of these accounts, except that you probably shouldn't to rely on one of these accounts for running a business, as they are not as flexible or reliable. The main advantage, though, is that they are perfect for if you are travelling or if you are only an occasional mail user. There have also been security problems with some of them, most notably Hotmail, although its owner Microsoft has now pledged all problems have now been fixed. When you are making your choice, you should always refer to the company's privacy policy as they are worth a read, even though they may be on the dull side. It is also worth checking that the company who owns your e-mail address cannot sell your details or e-mail address on. You may also have to pay for the more interesting facilities available. Some companies have useful features, such as signature, personalised e-mails, choice of domain name and holiday reply. All of which can be handy, but it depends on what your needs may be. All free sites are permanent and strictly not for business use. The most important aspects boil down to how often you can get logged on and how fast your mail is sent and received. If you want to be one of the more frugal users of e-mail and save yourself some money, then make sure you're reading and writing messages off-line. In other words, you dial up your e-mail provider, open your mailbox then disconnect from the Net again until you have read your emails and your responses. Most mail programs will let you 'Queue' a whole bunch of messages before sending them off, so you should do that if you can and then only when you've finished and queued up as much mail as you want to send, connect back up to the net and send them all. On some e-mail systems, and on many of the world wide web-based ones, you can't access the message creation when off-line. But you can, of course, type up and prepare your message in a text editor (like wordpad or notepad) while you are off-line and then simply cut and paste it into the message box when you go online. Don't rely on e-mail to get to your recipient immediately, although it usually does. If it's something urgent, you may have to go back to using the phone instead. The message is usually sent pretty quickly – more than 90 per cent arrive within five minutes – but the person you sent it to may not check their messages for hours and may not even be online at that point. All kinds of other factors can affect how quickly your mail is read, from how fast your ISP is connected to the rest of the Net, to simple things like the time difference between here and the US - if you are mailing in the morning, they may not get it until they wake up in the afternoon.

Many accounts, and all the main types of e-mail software allow you to set up one or more standard signatures which can be included at the end of every message saving you time. You can include your own contact details in your signature, for example, so you don't have to add them in every time.

Something to look out for in your e-mails...

In general, if someone mails you something with the message "Please forward this to all your friends" you really shouldn't. Even if it looks like an urgent virus warning, you should check with your company or with your ISP to check if there actually IS a virus warning. Everyone gets these chain letters and emotional blackmails which circulate round the Net all the time. Even if they have no basis in fact they do tend to panic people, so check whether it's yet another hoax before you hit that send button 'just in case' – it could actually BE a virus!

What on earth is spamming?!

The term spamming, or unsolicited e-mail is the e-mail equivalent of bulk junk mail. It is becoming more and more common and is extremely tedious for most users. The best thing to do is simply delete such mails and never reply to them, not even to a 'remove' address, which is used to good effect on mailing lists – it shows that you have taken time to reply to them! This will therefore simply get you added onto the list of 'live' and 'active' addresses, and you'll only get more. So before you open up any intriguingly titled mail (such as 'love letter', or 'make money fast' or 'find love') think carefully as to whether you recognise the senders address. If you don't, simply hit delete. If your net access lies behind a firewall (a filter), or your ISP is as keen as you are to filter such mail, you may never be troubled by spamming, but otherwise you are more or less bound to come across them at some point.

Chapter 11
Sending and Receiving E-mail

How do I actually send an e-mail?
Your browser makes it easy to send e-mail messages to others. You can either create a new message or you can use a link on the web, whether it is a page or a web site to open a new mail which will send the web page along with it to the page owner. To send someone a message, simply type his or her e-mail address in the 'To' field of a new e-mail message. In the case of emails, you need to have the address of the person you wish to send it to. You can also send one message to several people at once. To do this, you simply type the e-mail address of every person you want to receive the message, separated by a semicolon (;) in the 'To' field of your e-mail message. You can also type any additional e-mail addresses in the CC (carbon copy) or BCC (blind carbon copy) fields. This will have the same effect – it will send an exact copy of the mail to each person whose address

is typed there. You can also send documents and other files to people using e-mail.

How do I create an e-mail message?

It is different depending on who your e-mail provider is, but if you click your mouse on 'mail' on your Internet tool bar, and then follow the directions that you are given, you can't really go far wrong.

Netscape Communicator uses the following guidelines; From the Communicator menu (on some Macs, this menu appears as a small lighthouse icon), select Messenger, then Messenger Mailbox, or Messenger Inbox, depending on which version of Communicator you are using. Then click the New Msg button and a Message Composition window will appear. now, all you have to do is type your message in the large field at the bottom of the Message Composition window. Type a short (less than 10 words) title that describes the content of your e-mail in the Subject field. You now have to enter the recipients' e-mail addresses in the To, CC, or BCC fields, as above. Now, simply click the Send button and the e-mail will go to everyone who you typed in the fields at the top.

Sending and Receiving E-mail

On Internet Explorer/Outlook Express;
Firstly, click the Mail button on your browser toolbar (keep your mouse button pressed down if you're using a Mac computer). In the menu that will appear, choose New Message. Your e-mail program, Outlook Express, will open with a new, blank message window for you to begin. Now, type your message in the large field at the bottom of the New Message window. (If you have created an e-mail signature, it appears inside the message window at this point). Now, type a short (less than 10 words) title that describes the content of your e-mail in the Subject field. Then enter the recipients' e-mail addresses in the To, CC, or BCC field.

Then you simply have to click the Send or Send Now button for your e-mail to go.

If you are sending e-mail from World wide web pages;
Many World wide web pages let you send e-mail to the page's author, a mailing list, or other recipients using special HTML tags. When you click one of these tags, your browser automatically opens a pre addressed e-mail message. Simply type your message inside the message window, add a title, and click Send Now or Send.

How do I retrieve my e-mails?

To retrieve your new e-mails, your computer must connect to the Earth Link mail server and copy the new messages to your hard drive. Most e-mail programs will display messages in the order they arrived in your inbox. Depending on how your e-mail program is set, the newest messages will probably be either at the top or bottom of your inbox. Each e-mail message is displayed with a summary that includes its subject or title, the name of the sender, and the date (and sometimes the time) it was sent. Follow the directions for your browser to learn how to receive and read new e-mail messages.

To do this on Netscape Communicator;
From the Communicator menu, click on Messenger Mailbox or Messenger Mailbox. (In Netscape 4.5 for Macintosh, the Communicator menu is represented by a small Netscape icon.)

   Now, click the Get Msg button. You may be asked for your Earth Link password before Communicator will download your new messages. The program copies any new messages and sends them to your Inbox. The names of new messages appear in bold type and messages you have read appear in plain text. you now choose a new message to read by clicking on it. You can read e-mail messages in their own windows or within the Inbox window.

Sending and Receiving E-mail

To read a message in its own window, double-click on the message name. When you have finished reading this message, click the message window close box to close it.

To read messages within the Inbox window, click on the blue triangle in the bottom-left corner of the window. The message then appears in the lower half of the Inbox window.

To read messages on Microsoft Internet Explorer;
Click on **Mail** from the Go menu (Windows) or click the Mail button (Macintosh) to open your Outlook Express account. Now click the Send and Receive button to get new mail. You may be asked for your Earth Link user name and password before Outlook will download any new messages. The program will then copy and send any new messages to your Inbox. Again, the names of new messages will appear in bold type and messages you have read appear in plain text. you can select a new message by clicking on it. You can read e-mail messages within the Inbox window or in their own windows.

To read messages within the Inbox window, click on the name of the message. Its contents appear in the lower half of the Inbox window.

To read a message in its own window, double-click on the message name. When you have finished reading this message, click the message window's close box to close it.

How do I add e-mail addresses to my address book?

Before you add a person's e-mail address to your address book, it is important to make sure that the address is correct, and also double-check it after you enter it into your address book. If you enter the address incorrectly, you may have trouble sending e-mail to this person in the future. After you store addresses in your address book, you can send emails by using your address book. Follow the directions for your browser, below.

On Netscape Communicator;
Firstly, choose Address Book from the Communicator menu. (On Macintosh, this menu is represented by a small Netscape icon.). now, click on New Card. This opens for you a blank address form. The form is divided into three tabs – General, Contact, and Netscape Conference. Click the General tab. Now, type the person's full name in the First Name and Last Name blank spaces. Type the person's e-mail address in the E-mail blank. At this stage, you can enter an optional nickname for the person in the Nickname blank. Nicknames are typically a shorter version of the person's name that you can use when

Sending and Receiving E-mail

you are addressing their e-mail. For example, if the person's name is Alexander McDonald, enter Sandy or Alex in the Nickname field. You can then type Sandy instead of his full name when you are next sending him an e-mail. The recipient will see something like Sandy (Alexander McDonald) in his Inbox.

If you want to add a note to yourself about this address book entry, type it in the Notes field. For example, you can include the person's birthday or a reminder of where you met him or her. This information will not appear inside your e-mails. At the bottom of the window, there is a box marked Prefers to Receive HTML. When you check this box, the person you are e-mailing will receive HTML mail messages. Now click on the Contact tab. This tab lets you include optional contact information, which could include their company, phone and fax numbers, and address, for this person. None of this information will appear inside your e-mails. If this person has access to a Netscape Conference server, click Netscape Conference and enter the server address they in the field on this tab. Most people will never need to use this tab. Click on OK when you are finished making your changes to this entry.

On Internet Explorer/Outlook Express for Windows;
Firstly, choose Mail from the Go menu. Now, click

the Address Book button. On the window that appears, click New Contact. Type the person's name in the First, Middle, and Last blanks. Enter an optional nickname for the person in the Nickname blank. As above, nicknames are typically a shorter version of the person's name you can use when addressing his or her e-mail. For example, if the person's name is Alexander McDonald, you could enter Sandy or Alex in the Nickname field. You can then type Sandy instead of his full name when sending him e-mail. The recipient will see something like Sandy (Alexander McDonald) in his Inbox. Now, type the person's e-mail address in the Add new blank and press the Add button. If the person has more than one e-mail address, type the other address in Add new and press Add. After you click Add, the e-mail addresses appear in the large field at the bottom of the window. Select the e-mail address the person uses most often and click the Set as Default button. Click the Home, Business, and Other tabs to store contact information, including phone numbers, World wide web page addresses, work and home addresses, and job title, for this person. None of this information will appear inside your e-mails. If you or the person uses Microsoft NetMeeting conferencing software, click the NetMeeting tab and enter the person's conferencing e-mail address and **NetMeeting** server. If you or the recipient encrypt your mails

Sending and Receiving E-mail

with security filters, click the Digital IDs tab and click the Import button to assign a security certificate to this person's e-mail address. Press OK when you have finished making your changes to this entry.

On Internet Explorer/Outlook Express for Macintosh; Click the Mail button on your browser toolbar. Now, click the Contacts button. On the window that appears, click New. Type the person's name in the First Name and Last Name blanks. If the person is a business contact, type his or her title, company, and department in the appropriate blanks. Type the person's e-mail address in the E-mail Address blank and press the Add button. If the person has more than one e-mail address, type the other address in E-mail Address and press Add. After you click Add, the e-mail addresses appear in the field below E-mail Address. Select the e-mail address the person uses most often and click the Make Default button. If you want to save contact information, including phone numbers, World wide web page addresses, work and home addresses, and job title, for this person, type it in the Address and Phone Numbers areas. None of this information will appear inside your e-mails. If you want to add a note to yourself about this address book entry, type it in the large blank at the bottom of the window. For example, you can include the person's birthday or a reminder of where you met

141

him or her. This information will not appear inside your e-mails. Press Save when you are finished making your changes to this entry.

How do I send messages to people in my address book?

After you have saved the e-mail addresses of your family, friends, and business associates in your address book, you can easily send messages to them. You can either address your messages by typing the person's full name or their nickname (whatever appears in your address book) or send messages from inside your address book.

How to address messages to people listed in your address book . Follow the directions for your browser.

On Netscape Communicator;
Open a blank e-mail message by pressing Ctrl-M (Windows) or Command-M (Macintosh).

There are two ways to address messages to people in your address book -

Click inside the To box and type the person's name or nickname as it appears in the address book.

Click the Address button, select a recipient's name, and press To, CC, or BCC. Repeat this process to send to other people. Click OK when you're

Sending and Receiving E-mail

finished.

Now, type a subject, write your e-mail, and press Send.

On Internet Explorer/Outlook Express for Windows;
Choose Mail from the Go menu. Now, click Compose Message. There are two ways to address messages to people in your address book -

Click inside the To box and type the person's name or nickname as it appears in the address book.

Click the small index card icon next to To, select a recipient's name, and press To, CC, or BCC. Repeat this process to send to other people. Click OK when you're finished.

Now type a subject, write your e-mail, and press Send.

On Internet Explorer/Outlook Express for Macintosh;
Click the Mail button on your browser toolbar. Click the New button or press Command-N to open a new e-mail message. There are two ways to address messages to people in your address book -

Click inside the To box and type the person's name or nickname as it appears in the address book.

Click the Contacts button, select a person's name, and drag it into the To, CC, or BCC blank. Repeat this process to send to other people. Close the Contacts window when you're finished

Now, type a subject, write your e-mail, and press Send.

How to send messages from your address book
Follow the directions for your browser.

On Netscape Communicator;
Choose Address Book from the Communicator menu. (On Macintosh, this menu is represented by a small Netscape icon.) Select the person to whom you want to send a message. Now, press the New Msg button. A new e-mail message window appears. To add another recipient, follow the directions as above. Now, simply type a subject, write your e-mail, and press Send.

On Internet Explorer/Outlook Express for Windows;
Choose Mail from the Go menu. Click Address Book. Select the person to whom you want to send a message. Press the Send Mail button. A new e-mail message window appears.

To add another recipient, follow the directions as above. Type a subject, write your e-mail, and press Send.

On Internet Explorer/Outlook Express for Macintosh;
Click the Mail button on your browser toolbar. Click

Sending and Receiving E-mail

Contacts. Select the person to whom you want to send a message. Press the Mail To button. A new e-mail message window appears.

To add another recipient, follow the directions as above. Now, simply type a subject, write your e-mail, and press Send.

Setting up personal mailing lists

We have previously touched on how and why you may set up a mailing list for educational purposes. You may find that you often send the same messages to more than person. Perhaps you are chatting with the same group of friends, or you are sending a newsletter to clients. If so, you should set up one or more mailing lists to handle these groups of addresses. Each list can have a unique theme — family, friends, or business, for example — and addresses can appear in several lists. After you've established a list, you can easily send e-mail to the whole group at once. Simply replace the list of e-mail addresses in the To field with the name of the list, and hit Send. Your e-mail program will automatically send the message to every address on the list. To set up a personal mailing list, first make sure you know the correct e-mail address for every person you want on the list add these addresses to your address book, then follow the directions for your browser.

On Netscape Communicator;
Choose Address Book from the Communicator menu. (On Macintosh, this menu is represented by a small Netscape icon.) Click New List. This opens a window with spaces for you to enter the list's name, information about it, and the e-mail addresses you want on it. Enter a name for the list in the List Name field. For example, if you wanted to make a list of all your family's e-mail addresses, you might name it Family Members. Enter an optional nickname in the List Nickname box. A nickname is a shorter, easy-to-remember name you can use instead of the full name. Enter an optional description of the list in the Description box to help you remember why these people are grouped together. To add a name to the list, click the address book window to bring it to the front. Select the name you want to add. Drag the name into the bottom field of the New List window. The name will be added to the list. Repeat this process until you've added all the names you want on the list. Click OK to close and save the new list.

When you have established a list, you can edit it by double-clicking its name and dragging names in and out of it.

On Internet Explorer/Outlook Express for Windows;
Choose Mail from the Go menu. Click the Address Book button. On the window that appears, click New

Sending and Receiving E-mail

Group. Enter a name for the list in the List Name field. For example, if you wanted to make a list of all your family's e-mail addresses, you might name it Family Members. Click Select Members to add e-mail addresses from your address book. On the window that appears, select the person's name and click the Select button. Repeat until you've added all the names you want on the list, then press OK. If you want to remove an address from the list, click the name you want to remove and press the Remove button. Enter an optional description of the list in the Notes box to help you remember why these people are grouped together. Click OK to close and save the new list.

After you have established a list, you can edit it by double-clicking its name and using the Select Members and Remove buttons to add or remove members.

On Internet Explorer/Outlook Express for Macintosh; Click the Mail button on your browser toolbar. Click the Contacts button. On the window that appears, click Mailing List. The left side of the window will now display a small Contacts icon (it looks like an open book) and a Mailing List icon. Type a name for the new mailing list. Click the small Contacts icon to view the list of e-mail addresses in your address book. Select a person you want to add to this mailing list. Click and drag the person's name over the new mailing list's name. Repeat with other addresses you want to add to the mailing list. When you are finished, close the Contacts window. After you have established a list, you can edit it by double-clicking its name and dragging names in and out of it.

What is an e-mail signature?
Many frequent e-mail users will create and save a "signature file" that may include their name and other information about them (address, phone, a favourite quote, and so on). Netscape Communicator and Microsoft Internet Explorer automatically add this signature to the end of each e-mail message you send.

To create a signature file, type the information you want to use into a text editor like Notepad (Windows) or SimpleText (Macintosh). Although you can design your signature any way you like – and many people get very creative with them – it's probably best if signatures don't exceed eight lines. Save your signature on your hard drive. If you later want to change your signature, open the text file and type your new message. Remember to save the file after you make your changes.

Sending and Receiving E-mail

How do I reply to my e-mails?

With e-mail, it's easy to reply quickly to messages you receive. You can choose to reply only to the sender, or to the sender and all the other recipients of the message. A copy of the original message is included in each reply, which helps put your reply in context. After a while, one e-mail message may include several replies, so it's important to realise that the most recent reply that was sent will appear at the top, and the original mail will be at the bottom.

Follow the directions for your browser to learn how to reply to the original sender or to the sender as well as all other recipients.

On Netscape Communicator/Messenger for Windows;
Open the e-mail message you want to reply to. Click Reply and choose Reply to Sender from the drop-down menu. An e-mail message addressed to the sender opens. Type your reply in this window and press Send.

On Netscape Communicator/Messenger for Macintosh;
Open the e-mail message you want to reply to. Click Reply. An e-mail message addressed to the sender opens. Type your reply in this window and press Send.

On Internet Explorer/Outlook Express for Windows;
Open the e-mail message you want to reply to. Click Reply to Author. An e-mail message addressed to the sender opens. Type your reply in this window and press Send.

On Internet Explorer/Outlook Express for Macintosh;
Open the e-mail message you want to reply to. Click Reply. An e-mail message addressed to the sender opens. Type your reply in this window and press Send.

Be very careful when replying to the sender and all recipients as it is very possible that your reply may go to dozens of people at once. Limit your response to only the people who really need to see your reply.

On Netscape Communicator/Messenger for Windows;
Click Reply and choose Reply to Sender and All Recipients from the drop-down menu. An e-mail message addressed to every person who received the original e-mail opens. Type your reply in this window and press Send.

On Netscape Communicator/Messenger for Macintosh;
Click and hold the Reply button. Choose to Sender and All Recipients from the drop-down menu. An e-mail message addressed to every person who

Sending and Receiving E-mail

received the original e-mail opens. Type your reply in this window and press Send.

On Internet Explorer/Outlook Express for Windows; Click Reply to All. An e-mail message addressed to every person who received the original e-mail opens. Type your reply in this window and press Send.

On Internet Explorer/Outlook Express for Macintosh; Click Reply All. An e-mail message addressed to every person who received the original e-mail opens. Type your reply in this window and press Send.

Messages with multiple replies

Although your first e-mail message may look like a conventional typewritten letter, the unique nature of e-mail often turns a single message into a conversation. This is how and why it happens – you may send an e-mail message. Then, you get a reply to that message. The original message will still appear in the reply, with added questions and comments from the new sender. You will then respond to that response, and so on. At each step, the new message (the reply) is added to all the previous messages. This is how e-mail messages can get confusing, especially when they're sent to more than one person and each person responds.

It is worth noting that every time someone replies to a message, an angle bracket > is placed before each line. When someone replies to your reply, the original message gets two brackets >>, your reply to her gets one and the new message has no angle brackets. Some mail programs help clarify replies by inserting text before each quoted message to indicate who wrote the message, like this:

At 3:45 PM 11/15/96, John Smith wrote:

Another way to simplify an e-mail exchange is to delete unnecessary parts of earlier messages. There are no set rules for organising an e-mail conversation, but these few suggestions will make your messages more readable.

How can I attach files to my e-mail messages?

Netscape Communicator and Microsoft Outlook Express will let you attach files and entire World wide web pages to any e-mail message. This makes it easy for you to share pictures, documents, and your favourite sites with others. When an e-mail containing an attachment is delivered, the recipient receives a copy of the attached files.

On Netscape Communicator;
Netscape Communicator lets you attach files, World wide web pages, and personal address book cards to

Sending and Receiving E-mail

your e-mail messages. Choose Messenger Mailbox from the Communicator menu. (On Macintosh, the Communicator menu is represented by a small Netscape logo.) This opens your Inbox window. Click the New Msg button to open a new e-mail message. Click the Attach button. This opens a pop-up window that lets you attach a file, World wide web page, and/or your address book card. If you choose File, Communicator asks you to find the file you want to attach on your computer. Click once on the file's name and press the Open button to attach the file. If you choose World wide web page, the program will ask you for the URL of the page you wish to attach. You can attach any World wide web page, but be sure you type the URL correctly. If you choose Address book card, Communicator will include a file that contains the name, e-mail address, and other contact information you entered when you set up your e-mail program. Now, address the e-mail, write a message, and click Send to send your message.

On Internet Explorer for Windows;
Internet Explorer for Windows lets you send files and World wide web pages to others.

From the Go menu, select Mail. On the window that opens, click Compose Message. This opens a new message window. Select the message window's

Insert and choose File Attachment. Find the file you wish to attach in the dialogue box that opens. Click once on the file's name and press the Attach button to attach the file. The file's icon appears at the bottom of the e-mail message window. Address the e-mail, write a message, and click Send to send your message.

Sending World wide web pages;
Go to the World wide web page you want to send. From the File menu, choose Send. This opens a pop-up menu. Select Page by E-mail to send a copy of the page via e-mail. Select Link by E-mail to simply send a World wide web link to this page. Internet Explorer will create a new e-mail message containing your attachment. Address the e-mail, write a message, and click Send to send your message.

On Internet Explorer for Macintosh;
Internet Explorer for Macintosh lets you send files and World wide web pages to others. Click the Mail button to open Outlook Express. On the window that appears, click New to open a new e-mail message. Click the Add Attachments button. Find the file you wish to attach in the dialogue box that opens. Click once on the file's name and press the Add button to attach the file. To add every file in a folder, press Add All. After you add the file to your

Sending and Receiving E-mail

message, its name appears in the field at the bottom of the Add Attachments window. When you are finished adding files, press Done. Address the e-mail, write a message, and click Send to send your message.

Sending World wide web pages;
Go to the World wide web page you want to send. From the File menu, choose Save As and save the World wide web page on your hard drive. After saving the page as a file on your computer, follow the directions above to send the file.

Sorting e-mail messages as they arrive!

Your e-mail program can actually be set up to sort out mail into folders, before you have read them. This may be done by using a person's name that has sent the mail, or it could be based on the subject of the mail? This is another great advantage of e-mail – your postal mailbox can't do this, but your e-mail program can use filters to sort and organise your e-mail before you even open it. E-mail filters are commands that tell your e-mail program how to deal with incoming mail. Each filter consists of two things – a string of text or numbers and instructions on what to do with messages that contain this word or phrase. Filters primarily work on message headers –

the section of each e-mail that contains information about the sender, the recipient, the date of the message, and its subject. When you receive new e-mail, your browser compares the new messages' headers to your filters. If a message contains text or numbers you have selected to filter, the e-mail program follows the instructions for that filter.

Typically, filters are used to delete unwanted messages, to redirect certain kinds of messages into designated mailboxes, or to raise the priority of some messages so that you are sure to notice important e-mails.

Using a mailing list

Mailing lists are a form of e-mail which allow the user to communicate with all the other subscribers in one go instead of having to send individual messages one at a time to each user. Instead of posting a message to a person, a message is posted to the list address and is distributed to all the members of the list. This can be used to great effect when we use the example of students and employees. E-mail has suddenly given these individuals the chance to have a voice that can be heard – they are being encouraged to give feedback to various tutors or managers and feel as if they will at last have some form of input into various aspects of their career or course they are studying. Students especially used to play a passive role in their studies, by listening to the tutor and carrying out any tasks they were asked to do. Now, however, they can actively participate with lecturers, tutors and with other students who they may never actually have met. This is because of the immediate and active properties of the use of e-mail.

Creating a mailing list

Individuals and companies who do not have a mail server can take advantage of one of the free world wide web based e-mail services that are available through most ISPs and search engine sites, such as Hotmail, Yahoo!, AOL and Lycos. You can register for an account and carry out all the normal functions of conventional e-mail accounts, such as dealing with attachments, subscribing to mailing lists and so on, through a world wide web interface. The increasing use of e-mail means that mailing lists in a classroom situation are more and more becoming an accessible form of teaching. There are several ways to set up a list. The Mailbase group will set lists up with no charge for academic purposes, subject to the approval of short description of the list's purpose submitted to them. Another way to do this is to search the world wide web for a company that will set up a list for you. Generally all you will have to do is give the name and address of the person who will be in charge of the list, then you would e-mail anyone you wish to be on the list, and they will subscribe to that list through the world wide web. This means that there are no problems with people having a note of your e-mail address if you do not wish it to be of public use – the only person who has your e-mail address is the Internet company who is handling your mailing list.

Tips for a successful list

There are some things which should be considered when setting up a list to ensure that it is effective in achieving its purpose -
You should identify who you wish to be able to subscribe to your list – is it open to anyone or can anyone join if they wish to. In other words, is the list to be open or restricted? The second point to consider is if the list is for any purpose, i.e. is it just for social reasons, or does it have a specific purpose, such as discussing your favourite movies? You should then consider setting some guidelines and boundaries as to what is acceptable and what is not, and then send your first e-mail to the mailing list to explain these guidelines. The rules may simply define topics that you can or cannot discuss on the list.

You should then begin to publicise your list,

Sending and Receiving E-mail

unless the list is set up for a discrete group. Your purpose is to attract users and a membership for the list that you have decided to set up. Publicity, such as posting information to related lists or news groups, inclusion of the list address in a business card or letterhead, and word of mouth, should be done at every opportunity both when the list is set up and at regular intervals once the list is up and running, so you can continue to run your list successfully. If you are using a Mailbase list there is also the Mailbase link which displays all new lists to which you can submit information about your list.

Finally, you should be able to begin a discussion! Unless the purpose of the list is educational, and so participation is compulsory, you should take some time to encourage contributions from all of your members. You should be able to encourage the active members by making relevant responses to their messages wherever possible. If someone does not contribute much, make a fuss of them when they finally do, but replying to them and encouraging further discussion. You may want to make it a list policy that new members introduce themselves and give a brief description of their areas of interest and their reasons for joining the list. This will give a pointer as to topics that others may wish to discuss with them.

Anecdotal evidence suggests that a substantial

percentage of list members will not be active in the list discussions at all. A term used to describe such a person is a lurker. The lurker who subscribes to the list and perhaps reads all the postings, but never makes a contribution, will be a familiar figure to anyone who manages a list of any size. Even the lurker, however, will find some benefit from their membership of the list. They will learn, if only in the more traditional sense of a passive way to receive and acquire knowledge rather than being actively engaged in the production of knowledge.

Chapter 12
Using the World Wide Web as a Teaching Tool

The Internet as used in Schools

If you are a teacher, or are interested in school education, you've probably already begun to see the potential the Net has for use in the class room. Many programs and ISPs have tremendous educational potential, from keeping up with world events to arranging international science experiments. Because the Net now reaches - and is widely used - in so many countries and often stays online even when the phones go down, you and your students can log on to first-hand accounts from people involved in international conflicts. Look at your system's list of Usenet groups to see if there is one available about the country or region that you are interested in. Even in peacetime when there are no conflicts happening, these news groups can be great places to find people from countries you might be studying.

Why Use the World wide web?

The simple fact of the matter is that the world wide web is one of the most educational tools we have available to us – and it is only the beginning. There is nothing that we can see or listen to that will not one day be available on the world wide web. In 1997, there were still some sceptics arguing that the World wide web was a transitory medium, enjoying over-hyped success. Indeed, many people wondered whether they should still be developing material using standard multimedia authoring packages in case they were to become obsolete. In the space of two years, it is clear that these doubts have disappeared and that they were in fact unjustified. The explosion of the world wide web into popular culture and acceptance is unquestioned and indeed unquestionable. The power of the World wide web in terms of reaching the general public in the developed world has been shown in many ways. They range from educational purposes, for instance satellite pictures of the landings on the Space Station, and political - the recent publication of the Starr Report - to the downright worrying, such as the increase in pornography and paedophilia. The World wide web is one of the most accessible tools available for academics to use. It allows easy access of publishing material, it has a low learning-curve, the majority of its browsers are graphic and very user-friendly, and

Using the WWW as a Teaching Tool

above all it is free to most people in Higher Education, due to the facilities now offered to students in schools and colleges. As we have already outlined, the World wide web works on a client-server principle. The user boots up their browser - Netscape or Internet Explorer - on their computer, which in turn asks a server to retrieve it some files. Files are located through their Uniform Resource Locator (URL) or world wide web site address - a unique address detailing the protocol for transferring the data, the domain name of the World wide web server, and the path name/filename of the actual document.

Resource-Based Learning In Schools and Colleges

We have already discussed the use of student-centred resource-based learning. The purpose of this being that students need access to greater resources to use and discuss for their learning, or research, and today's technology has the ability to achieve this goal.

The World wide web can be viewed as one enormous resource that is inter linked, but is always expanding. The problem is therefore not really the lack of resources, but is more that of locating them from the hundreds of other sites on the world wide web. There are two approaches to solving this problem which have developed over the years.

The first is the use of gateways, the second the use of search engines.

Internet Gateway when used in Teaching

A gateway is a selected list of links which is categorised by subject and by subject category. The United Kingdom hosts several such gateways. The main gateways of use to us are;

- ADAM – Art, Design, Architecture & Media Information Gateway
- EEVL – Edinburgh Engineering Virtual Library
- HUMBUL – Humanities Bulletin Board
- IHR-Info – Institute for Historical Research Information
- OMNI – Organising Medical Networked Information
- SOSIG – Social Science Information Gateway

All of these gateways were funded under JISC's Electronic Libraries Programme, with the exception of HUMBUL which was funded by internal money within Oxford University. Some of them employ the ROADS system, which stands for Resource Organisation and Discovery in Subject-based services, which is aimed at managing the development of gateways, but undoubtedly all of them attempt to provide the main functions of a

Using the WWW as a Teaching Tool

gateway as listed above. They are a good starting point for students to look to as they are excellent collections of good educationally based links to relevant world wide web sites. In addition, the creation of World wide web Indexes, e.g. Yahoo! or Magellan, provide another entrance point to these virtual libraries. However, students may find Magellan a bit daunting as their coverage of subjects is very extensive but their selection method is not always made clear. The advantage of the gateways noted above lies in the method used in the selection of resources. An enthusiast, a subject expert, or a librarian, bring their opinions and prejudices to the sites they link to.

Internet Search Engines

As we know, gateways are not the only way of locating existing world wide web pages, but they do provide the advantage of being subject specific. However, it is very possible that the Gateways in existence do not cover your subject area in any great detail. In addition to this, the topic you are interested in may be linked in some way to another major topic and thus primary research and teaching resources may be located elsewhere. Either way, at some point you will want to look at, or direct your students to, an Internet Search Engine.

Internet Search engines have existed since the early days of the World wide web. They employ programs called Robots or World wide web Crawlers to search for and index new world wide web pages and sites. The index database can then be queried through a World wide web form on the search engine. Many search engines support a sophisticated query language based on Boolean theories, which allow users to narrow their searches down to a fine degree, keeping wasted links to a minimum. The main and most popular search engines in existence are;

- AltaVista
- HotBot
- InfoSeek
- Excite
- Lycos.

All of these are very powerful tools, but at the same time vary in and coverage. The main problem with search engines is the misuse of them by users. That is to say that search requests are often too vague or too open, which results in bringing back thousands of possible links. For this reason alone it is essential that students who are directed to search engines as a means of research have been taught how to search effectively, as outlined previously in the book. Many users clearly do not know how to use the query language which is used in most search engines. This then results in them becoming discouraged when the first few pages of search results offer them very little of any interest to them. Things are made much easier by Meta search engines which send a user's query to a number of different search engines, collect and compare the results, and remove any sites that are of no use. Nevertheless the process of finding useful information can account for a significant proportion of the user's online time.

Navigating the World wide web

Before we move on to looking at the types of things that tutors are using the World wide web for in teaching, it is a useful point to confront some of the common problems that users of the World wide web, and in particular beginners, come across. The World wide web works under a hypertext metaphor, in other words it operates via a series of nodes and links. A user can be looking for a piece of information and when they see a link they can simply activate and open it by clicking on it. At this point, some other node of information, e.g. a document, will be retrieved. Hypertext, as a teaching tool, has been viewed for many years as being potentially very useful. This is because a book, for instance, does not give the opportunity within itself to be cross-referenced or to be questioned. If a book is used in a class, there will obviously be students of many different academic levels, and so the book will not have an equal impact on all of the students. The Internet and the world wide web, though, gives students the chance to question the author, to find information on the subject for themselves and allows the student to be motivated by themselves, or for them to be directed by their tutor or lecturer. As with most areas of the Internet and the world wide web, there are problems with all of this.

One such problem, in fact is that there is so much information available to the students that they may face overloading of information which they do not know how to sort out into importance and usefulness. This in itself with cause frustration and discouragement. It is generally considered that when users move around a large information space as much as they do in hypertext and on the world wide web, there is a real risk that they may become lost or have trouble finding the information they need. Even a small document, which could be read in one hour, can cause users to experience the problem of being completely lost in cyberspace. The problem really is that if you don't read or save something when you come across it you may, depending on the subject you are reading, never find it again because of the

Using the WWW as a Teaching Tool

vast amount of information available.

Therefore, when the world wide web is being used for educational purposes, the lecturer or teacher has to focus the student and point them to the specific area of learning. It is not a simple matter of presenting the student with a search engine and telling them to get on with it. Confusion is as much a disadvantage in learning as not being given enough information. That is not to say that the World wide web or World wide web browsers do not come complete with useful tools which offer great help. They all come will toolbars which offer standard navigational buttons, History lists, Backtrack facilities, and Bookmarks.

What is hypertext?

Most of the protocols that existed before the World wide web were very boring to look at, even if the information was sometimes quite fascinating. There were no diagrams, no font types and no photographs. It was often difficult to find what you were looking for unless you knew exactly what you were looking for – there were no search engines as we know them today, so it was all down to knowing the address of the site you were looking for. E-mail was probably the first Internet protocol that had a major appeal for very obvious reasons, but it was still basically text with no special formatting or pictures. This is basically what the Internet used to look like.

The HTTP protocol and the World wide web came along and changed everything that had been known before. These colourful and exciting files of information are called hypertext which is how world wide web pages are created and developed. It is basically the language that is used.

It is known as "hyper"text because of its very useful ability to;

- offer built-in links to other sections of the same document
- or other documents on the same site…

The choice of which direction the text would take was increasingly becoming under the control of the reader and the user. The word "interactive" started to be used to describe this. It is now a word that is commonly used throughout the world.

An early hypertext link would appear on the screen as an underlined word.

When hypertext is combined with the world-wide Internet through the HTTP protocol, links can not only branch off to sections of the same document, but by clicking selected areas of a www hypertext document, you are virtually sent across the Internet via HTTP to one server after another. Because of the

"HT" part of HTTP, almost anyone can navigate through cyberspace through the World wide web.

The form of hypertext used on the world wide web is called "HTML" which stands for hypertext Mark-up Language. It's actually a spin-off of another mark-up language called SGML. The earliest and basic forms of HTML didn't look too much different from basic world wide web pages that you will see today – those without pictures and images. The main difference is the links that appear on many of these pages – they would not have been present many years ago.

Chapter 13
Starting and Designing your own World Wide Web pages

What does HTML do?
HTML files are basically simple text files that include tags which the world wide web browser uses to format the text and page. Using these tags and other special compressed graphics files called GIFs and Jpegs, images can be added and saved into the display Using a thing called the common gateway interface or CGI, servers could also take specific input from forms which are also built into the HTML documents, and create databases, send e-mail, create new HTML documents on the fly and other tricks!

More tools that are used...
Java: HTML can also contain tags that use a programming language called Java, which allows servers to send little programs to your computer to

run right in your world wide web browser.

VRML: By linking to documents of another mark-up language called virtual reality mark-up language or VRML, three-dimensional-seeming objects and places can be illustrated in world wide web pages. This is very useful, especially for educational purposes – there may be a place that you will never go to, but you can visit that place through the use of 3-D pictures on the Net. Another useful way to use this is through maps – it is always easier to understand how a landscape will look in real life if you can see the map in three dimensions, rather than on a flat piece of paper.

Another interesting and very useful feature of HTML is that it can also link to most of the pre-existing Internet protocols, as well. A good world wide web browser can also send e-mail and FTP requests. Some can even open a program which will allow you to log on to other computers and have a chat.

Is there more to the World Wide Web than http:// ?

Yes. Even though http is very stylish and can undertake many exciting tasks and features, there are other tools that can be used. There are many other protocols which have their own advantages and

Starting and Designing your own WWW pages

disadvantages, but many can add to the http:// possibilities.

The Gopher protocol will let you search for specific files that may be of use to you. And this Gopher doesn't harbour unrequited secret and passionate longing for Julie the Cruise Director.

"Alex" is the gopher that is shared by such diverse businesses as North Carolina State, in the US and Oxford in England. The news protocol allows to send questions and comments to many groups of people interested in a specific topic. There are literally thousands of different groups available. It then gives you the opportunity to download and read other peoples comments and questions. Again, this can be a situation where there are many meaningless comments from people who have nothing better to do, but there are often comments worth reading.

Is there more to the Internet that the World Wide Web?

Yes, there is, as briefly discussed previously. But the www is one of the easiest and most comfortable ways of using the Internet. Some of you may wonder why you would want to leave the comfort of your world wide web browser and look for something else to do on the Net, but there are a variety of things you can go to which you may not have previously thought of.

Some have been discussed already in this book, but it is worth summarising everything together, for ease of reference. Here are some of the other things that you can do with your Internet account. You will be able to carry out many of these features with your browser, such as the use of e-mail, but you will need extra software for some other things.

E-mail, or electronic mail, is still the most widely used tool on the Internet. Most world wide web browsers, including both Internet Explorer and Netscape, can handle most e-mail tasks these days, as they are constantly being updated and adapted to rectify any problems people have encountered. Some people prefer to have a separate e-mail program, such as Eudora. The e-mail program Telnet allows you to log onto other computers for a variety of reasons. The most basic use of Telnet is to log on to a bulletin board system or BBS. Not all BBSs have Internet gateways, but more and more do as they are developed. A BBS is a computer that may have information, forums, file areas and chat rooms. If you like talking to people with a sense of anonymity, then telnet will allow you to do just that. Some operating systems like Windows 95 come with a Telnet client already installed, so it is worth checking this in your user manual before you pay more money for something that you really did not need, as all computers and all systems are different.

Starting and Designing your own WWW pages

FTP, or File Transfer Protocol, is possibly the quickest way to move files around the Internet. Most browsers will support most FTP requests, but for anyone serious about creating a world wide web site, a good stand alone FTP client is a must as it will be able to carry much more information and will do this in a fraction of the time.

The IRC (Internet Relay Chat) is a vast network of chat rooms, where you'll find people communicating by keyboard on topics that range from philosophical to political to mundane to anything that you wish to begin discussing. The IRC is huge, and also has many sites that would shock you, so you should be very cautious with regards to allowing children to use them – at least you should always supervise them if they are being used. A Finger client is a tool that will allow you to have a look into other systems and see who is currently logged in. Many systems, though, do not have a finger server that will let just anybody in and some have finger servers that are much more indiscreet, shall we say. The output you receive from a finger request varies from domain to domain. One site could tell you all about an individual who is currently chatting, such as their e-mail address, and another could simply tell you their nickname and where in the world they are logged on.

This is by no means a complete list. More and

more interesting uses of the Internet are appearing literally every day. Cybercasting of both video and audio, both one-way and two way, are closer and closer to being used by the general public and many people are already doing it.

Where can I get Internet software?
The following sites are mainly based in the US, but they are accessible by all of us, and all have various interesting features. Some of them have all sorts of software available and some have only Internet software.

- Windows (95 and 3.1)
- Tucows
- The Internet Hotel
- Windows (95 and NT)
- www.32BIT.com
- Windows 95
- www.Windows95.com
- Macintosh
- The Mac Software Catalogue
- Amiga
- Aminet

Starting and Designing your own WWW pages

How can I start to build my own World Wide Web site?

Once you begin to feel more confident about using the Internet and the www, you may feel that you would like to build your own basic world wide web site so that you can get deeper into the world of the Internet. To establish a presence for yourself on the Internet, a world wide web site is a must. When you sign up with an Internet service provider, check what comes with the account. Many Internet accounts come with a few megabytes of space to let you store a world wide web site and allow you to FTP to that space to put your world wide web pages there, modify them and take them down again. The chances are that you or somebody you know already has a space for a world wide web site that is sitting there completely empty. It is worth doing, even if it is just for your own use, to allow you to get to know the ins and outs of the Internet. Once you have a place to put your world wide web site, you can begin the process of creating it.

HTML is not as difficult as you may first imagine, but it does take effort and learning to be able to use it effectively. There are many sites in the world wide web that will allow you to learn these basics and will teach you as much as you need to know to begin to build a basic world wide web site. They will teach you how to use and create HTML and will let you learn how it works and why.

The NCSA offers a site called "A Beginner's Guide to HTML".

Netscape offers an attractive site called Creating Net Sites. This is a very colourful and simple way to learn about HTML, and is possibly a good place to begin, as it doesn't look daunting or confusing.

Finally, there is a site called How to create a World wide web Page. Again, it is a very useful site which covers all the basics, as well as covering important points in some depth.

Many of these sites also have links which will allow you to e-mail the creator of the site and they will give you some pointers as to how to get started, or to help you create documents and text to get a good start. Some companies may charge you to do this, some may not, so check what you are getting from them before you pay them! It is also a good method to use, as they will be able to add diagrams and illustrations to the text that you have already created for use on your site.

How can my World Wide Web site work for me?

Once you have created your world wide web site, no matter how basic or unimportant it may be, you will want people to see it! A good idea to begin, if your site is business-related, is to display the world wide

Starting and Designing your own WWW pages

web address on other stationary, such as on your business cards, newspaper advertisements, letter heads and posters. An interesting point is that many companies have a world wide web site that simply shows you all the information that has already been given to you in the form of a leaflet or an advert or poster. In other words, they are not adding to or enhancing their service to their customers by simply showing them what they can already see elsewhere. To use the Internet and the world wide web to reach even more people, your site should offer visitors something interesting to do or learn once they are there, or you may wish to offer a discount or a small free gift to any customers that have come to you through the world wide web site, as an incentive for them to take the time to do this.

To really expand your business market and get even more people to know about you, your site should also be promoted, if possible, from within the Internet itself. This means that you should have your URL submitted to the dozens of search engines like Yahoo or Alta Vista, so that when people are searching through the search engine, your world wide web page will be one that the engine offers its user to go to. To put it another way, there is no point if you have a world wide web site that offers customers some wonderful things, but you can only get to it if you know the world wide web address. It is therefore always worthwhile to contact the various search engines to submit your details to them. Your site should also be crafted in a way that allows search engines to point the right people to your site. It is also very worthwhile to try to find other sites that may be willing to include a link to your site. This may be a company that offers related products but is not in direct competition with you. For instance, a shop that sells flooring products such as carpets and tiles, may be willing to have a link to a site that sells paint and wall tiles. This can sometimes be done for free, but for the best results, it's best to find a few good sites that are generating a lot of traffic and offer to sponsor them in return for an area or an advert on their page that contains a link to your site.

Your world wide web site should also give people the opportunity to be able to get in touch with you if they wish to do so, whether it is to get more information from you or to buy something or even just to give you some feedback on how they found your site and what they thought of it. This should be made as easy as possible for them, or you may find that nobody takes the time to e-mail you at all. Feedback is almost as important as having a world wide web site at all. It is useful when customers let you know they were there at all. This facility should be done in a way that allows them to be downloaded as quickly as possible. High resolution graphics and

Starting and Designing your own WWW pages

lots of fancy photographs can make a world wide web site look very attractive and may encourage people to have a good look at your page, but if it takes a long time for these photos to download to your visitor's computer, the visitor may not even wait until the site has downloaded. They may simply cancel the instruction to the browser and start looking elsewhere. And once your visitor has already seen your photos and graphics and know what they look like, they do very little from that point on except drain the resources of the system, slow down the delivery of the actual content of your page and make your visitor become impatient and annoyed. This is never a good idea when it is so easy for them to go to the world wide web site of one of your competitors.

Hopefully, this has given you the pointers on how to begin researching and finding any information you might need to start to build and design your own world wide web site or world wide web page. There is simply far too much to go into for it all to be explained in this book, but when you start researching HTML, it will begin to become very clear as to how and where you can get support to begin.

Tips to consider when starting a World Wide Web site

One of the best rules I can give you when you are setting up your own world wide web page is that it is not always a good idea to have certain features on your world wide web site just because you know how to do this. Always try to think of the benefits of adding something to the site and why your customers would want you or not want you to have such a feature. For instance, don't have a logo that bounces around on the screen just because you know how to make it do this and because it looks good, because it may mean that it becomes annoying for the user and they may click "back" and begin on a competitor's world wide web site.

Rule number two would have to be that when things go wrong, it's usually something very simple that has caused this and don't panic!

Chapter 14
Glossary of terms used in this book and in user manuals

Access Provider
Company or a group of companies who sell Internet connections to both businesses and the general public. They are also known as ISPs or Internet service providers. A typical UK access provider is BT Internet at www.btinternet.com

Active X
Microsoft designed concept program that allows a program to run inside a world wide web page.

ADN (Advanced Digital Network)
Usually refers to a 56Kbps leased line.

ADSL (Asynchronous Digital Subscriber Line)
A broad band Internet connection which allows a faster connection speed.

Anonymous FTP

This message usually appears on your computer screen if there is a problem connecting to the server when you are trying to access a page or site on the Internet.

AOL

Acronym for America Online, which is now integrated into the Time Warner empire. It is an ISP which is used by vast amounts of people every day throughout the world.

Applet

A small Java program that can be embedded in an HTML page. Applets differ from fully fledged Java applications in that they are not allowed to access certain resources on the local computer, such as files and serial devices (modems, printers, etc..), and are prohibited from communicating with most other computers across a network. The current rule is that an applet can only make an Internet connection to the computer from which the applet was sent.

Archie

Type of software which will find files that are stored on anonymous FTP sites. You will need to know the exact file name or at least a sub string of it.

ARPANet (Advanced Research Projects Agency Network)

This is the system that was to become the Internet. It was developed in the late 60's and early 70's by the US Department of Defence as an experiment in wide area networking that would survive a nuclear war.

ASCII (American Standard Code for Information Interchange)

The world-wide standard for the code numbers used by computers to represent all the upper and lower-case Latin letters, numbers, punctuation, etc.. There are 128 standard ASCII codes each of which can be represented by a 7 digit binary number: 0000000 through 1111111. It is simply a text format which can be read by all computers to ensure compatibility. It is also sometimes known as plain text.

Backbone

A high-speed line or series of connections that forms a major pathway within a network. The term is relative as a backbone in a small network will likely be much smaller than many non-backbone lines in a large network.

Bandwidth

The size of the data network pipeline. It is really how much stuff you can send through a connection. It is usually measured in bits-per-second. A full page of English text is about 16,000 bits. A fast modem can move about 15,000 bits in one second. Full-motion full-screen video would require roughly 10,000,000 bits-per-second, depending on compression.

Baud Rate

The number of times per second the signal transmitted by a modem changes. In common usage the baud rate of a modem is how many bits it can send or receive per second. Technically, baud is the number of times per second that the carrier signal shifts value – for example a 1200 bit-per-second modem actually runs at 300 baud, but it moves 4 bits per baud (4 x 300 = 1200 bits per second). It should never be confused with bits per second, or BPS.

BBS

Abbreviation used for Bulletin Board System. It is a computerised meeting and announcement system that allows people to carry on discussions, upload and download files, and make announcements without the people being connected to the computer at the same time. There are many thousands of BBSs around the world – most are very small, running on a single IBM clone PC with 1 or 2 phone lines. Some are very large and the line between a BBS and a system like CompuServe gets crossed at some point, but it is not clearly drawn.

Binary File

Any file which contains more than just plain text, or ASCII.

Binary News Group

A Usenet group that is specifically meant for posting binary files.

Binhex

The short form used to describe BINary HEXadecimal. It is a method for converting non-text files (non-ASCII) into ASCII. This is needed because Internet e-mail can only handle items in ASCII.

Bit

Binary DigIT. It is a single digit number in base-2, in other words, either a 1 or a zero. It is basically the smallest unit of computerised data. Bandwidth is usually measured in bits-per-second.

BITNET

Acronym for one of two things – either Because It's Time NETwork or Because It's There NETwork. Whichever definition is used, it is a network of educational sites which are separate from the Internet, but e-mail is freely exchanged between BITNET and the Internet. Listservs, the most popular form of e-mail discussion groups, originated on BITNET. BITNET machines are usually mainframes running the VMS operating system, and the network is probably the only international network that is shrinking.

Bookmark

Used on Netscape to describe a page or site that has been saved for you to return to at any time with a single click of the mouse.

Boot Up

The start up procedure on a computer.

Bounced Mail

An e-mail that has not been taken and has been returned to the sender. This may have happened because the e-mail address is incorrect and has not been recognised by the server.

Glossary

Bps (Bits Per Second)
This is a measurement of how fast data is moved from one place to another, in other words between two modems. A 28.8 modem can move 28,800 bits per second.

Broad band
High speed Internet access.

Browser
Used on both Netscape and Internet Explorer. It is used to describe any program that will allow you to view the world wide web Client program (software) that is used to look at various kinds of Internet resources.

BTW (or By The Way)
This is a shorthand appended to a comment written in an online forum

Buffer
An area that is used for temporary storage of data.

Byte
A set of Bits that represent a single character. Usually there are 8 Bits in a Byte, sometimes more, depending on how the measurement is being made.

Cache

Temporary storage space. This stores copies of your most recently visited pages in the cache area. It is also known as temporary Internet files in Internet Explorer.

Certificate Authority

This is an issuer of Security Certificates used in SSL connections.

CGI (Common Gateway Interface)

This is a set of rules that describe how a World wide web Server communicates with another piece of software on the same machine, and how the other piece of software, the "CGI program", talks to the world wide web server. Any piece of software can be a CGI program if it handles input and output according to the CGI standard. Usually a CGI program is a small program that takes data from a world wide web server and does something with it, like putting the content of a form into an e-mail message, or turning the data into a database query. You can often see that a CGI program is being used by seeing "cgi-bin" in a URL, but not always.

cgi-bin

The most common name of a directory on a

world wide web server in which CGI programs are stored. The "bin" part of cgi-bin is a shorthand version of "binary", because once, most programs were referred to as binaries. In real life, most programs found in cgi-bin directories are text files, or scripts that are executed by binaries located elsewhere on the same machine.

Client

A software program that is used to contact and obtain data from a Server software program on another computer, often across a great distance. Each Client program is designed to work with one or more specific kinds of Server programs, and each Server requires a specific kind of Client. A World wide web Browser is a specific kind of Client.

co-location

This is most often used to refer to having a server that belongs to one person or group physically located on an Internet-connected network that belongs to another person or group. Usually this is done because the server owner wants their machine to be on a high-speed Internet connection and/or they do not want the security risks of having the server on their own network.

Cookie

A piece of information sent by a World wide web Server to a World wide web Browser that the Browser software is expected to save and to send back to the Server whenever the browser makes additional requests from the Server. Depending on the type of Cookie used, and the Browser's settings, the Browser may accept or not accept the Cookie, and may save the Cookie for either a short time or a long time. Cookies might contain information such as login or registration information, online "shopping cart" information, user preferences, etc.. When a Server receives a request from a Browser that includes a Cookie, the Server is able to use the information stored in the Cookie. For example, the Server might customise what is sent back to the user, or keep a log of particular user's requests. Cookies are usually set to expire after a predetermined amount of time and are usually saved in memory until the Browser software is closed down, at which time they may be saved to disk if their "expire time" has not been reached. Cookies do not read your hard drive and send your life story to the CIA, but they can be used to gather more information about a user than would be possible without them.

Glossary

Cyberpunk

Originally a cultural sub-genre of science fiction taking place in a not-so-distant over-industrialised society. The term grew out of the work of William Gibson and Bruce Sterling and has evolved into a cultural label encompassing many different kinds of human, machine, and punk attitudes. It includes clothing and lifestyle choices as well.

Cyberspace

Originated by author William Gibson in his novel *Neuromancer* – the word Cyberspace is currently used to describe the whole range of information resources available through computer networks.

Digerati

The digital version of literati, it is a reference to a vague cloud of people seen to be knowledgeable, hip, or otherwise in-the-know in regards to the digital revolution.

Domain Name

The term used to describe the unique name that identifies an Internet site. It is sometimes called a web address or internet address. Domain Names always have 2 or more parts, separated by dots. The part on the left is the most specific, and the part on the right is the most general. A given machine may have more than one Domain Name but a given Domain Name points to only one machine. For example, the domain names: yahoo.com, mail.yahoo.com, workshop.yahoo.com can all refer to the same machine, but each domain name can refer to no more than one address. Usually, all of the machines on a given Network will have the same thing as the right-hand portion of their Domain Names (yahoo.com in the previous examples). It is also possible for a Domain Name to exist but not be connected to an actual machine. This is often done so that a group or business can have an Internet e-mail address without having to establish a real Internet site. In these cases, some real Internet machine must handle the mail on behalf of the listed Domain Name.

DSL (Digital Subscriber Line)

A method for moving data over regular phone lines. A DSL circuit is much faster than a regular phone connection, and the wires coming into the subscriber's premises are the same (copper) wires used for regular phone service. A DSL circuit must be configured to connect two specific locations, similar to a leased line. A commonly discussed configuration of DSL allows downloads at speeds of up to 1.544 megabits (not megabytes) per second, and uploads at speeds of 128 kilobits per second. This arrangement is called ADSL: "Asymmetric" Digital Subscriber Line. Another common configuration is symmetrical: 384 Kilobits per second in both directions. In theory ADSL allows download speeds of up to 9 megabits per second and upload speeds of up to 640 kilobits per second. DSL is now a popular alternative to Leased Lines and ISDN, being faster than ISDN and less costly than traditional Leased Lines.

E-mail (Electronic Mail)

Messages which are usually made up of text, which are sent from one person to another via their computers. E-mail can also be sent automatically to a large number of addresses (see also MAILING LIST).

Ethernet

A very common method of networking computers in a LAN. Ethernet will handle about 10,000,000 bits-per-second and can be used with almost any kind of computer.

FAQ (Frequently Asked Questions)

FAQs are documents that list and answer the

most common questions on a particular subject. There are hundreds of FAQs on subjects as diverse as Pet Grooming and Cryptography on the web. FAQs are usually written by people who have tired of answering the same question over and over.

FDDI (Fibre Distributed Data Interface)

This is a standard for transmitting data on optical fibre cables at a rate of around 100,000,000 bits-per-second (10 times as fast as Ethernet, about twice as fast as T-3).

Finger

An Internet software tool for locating people on other Internet sites. Finger is also sometimes used to give access to non-personal information, but the most common use is to see if a person has an account at a particular Internet site. Many sites do not allow incoming Finger requests, but many do.

Fire Wall

A combination of hardware and software that separates a LAN into two or more parts for security purposes.

Flame

Originally, the term flame meant "to carry out in a

passionate manner the spirit of honourable debate". Flames most often involved the use of flowery language and flaming well was an art form. More recently flame has come to refer to any kind of derogatory comment on the internet , no matter how witless or crude.

Flame War

When an online discussion degenerates into a series of personal attacks against the debaters, rather than discussion of their positions. A flame war is a heated exchange.

FTP (File Transfer Protocol)

A very common method of moving files between two Internet sites. FTP is a special way to login to another Internet site for the purposes of retrieving and/or sending files. There are many Internet sites that have established publicly accessible repositories of material that can be obtained using FTP, by logging in using the account name anonymous, thus these sites are called anonymous ftp servers.

Gateway

The technical meaning is a hardware or software set-up that translates between two dissimilar protocols, for example Prodigy has a gateway that translates between its internal, proprietary e-mail format and Internet e-mail format. Another, sloppier meaning of gateway is to describe any mechanism for providing access to another system, e.g. AOL might be called a gateway to the Internet.

GIF (Graphic Interchange Format)

A common format for image files, especially suitable for images containing large areas of the same colour. GIF format files of simple images are often smaller than the same file would be if stored in JPEG format, but GIF format does not store photographic images as well as JPEG.

Gigabyte

1000 or 1024 Megabytes, depending on who is measuring.

Gopher

A widely successful method of making menus of material available over the Internet. Gopher is a Client and Server style program, which requires that the user have a Gopher Client program. Although Gopher spread rapidly across the globe in only a couple of years, it has been largely supplanted by Hypertext, also known as WWW (World wide web). There are still thousands of

Glossary

Gopher Servers on the Internet and we can expect they will remain for a while.

Hit

As used in reference to the World wide web, "hit" means a single request from a world wide web browser for a single item from a world wide web server; thus in order for a world wide web browser to display a page that contains 3 graphics, 4 "hits" would occur at the server: 1 for the HTML page, and one for each of the 3 graphics. "Hits" are often used as a very rough measure of load on a server, e.g. "Our server has been getting 300,000 hits per month." Because each "hit" can represent anything from a request for a tiny document (or even a request for a missing document) all the way to a request that requires some significant extra processing (such as a complex search request), the actual load on a machine from 1 hit is almost impossible to define.

Home Page

Originally, the world wide web page that your browser is set to use when it starts up. The more common meaning refers to the main world wide web page for a business, organisation, person or simply the main page out of a collection of world wide web pages, e.g. "have a look at so-and-so's new Home Page." Another use of the term refers to practically any world wide web page as a "home page," e.g. "That world wide web site has 65 home pages and none of them are interesting."

Host

Any computer on a network that is a repository for services available to other computers on the network. It is quite common to have one host machine provide several services, such as WWW and USENET.

HTML

Abbreviation for hypertext Mark-up Language. This is the name give to the coding language used to create Hypertext documents for use on the World wide web. HTML looks a lot like old-fashioned typesetting code, where you surround a block of text with codes that indicate how it should appear, additionally, in HTML you can specify that a block of text, or a word, is linked to another file on the Internet. HTML files are meant to be viewed using a World wide web Client Program, such as Netscape or Mosaic.

HTTP (hypertext Transfer Protocol)

This is the protocol for moving hypertext files

across the Internet. Requires a HTTP client program on one end, and an HTTP server program on the other end. HTTP is the most important protocol used in the World wide web (WWW).

Hypertext
Text that contains links to other documents - words or phrases in the document that can be chosen by a reader and which cause another document to be retrieved and displayed.

IMHO (In My Humble Opinion)
This is shorthand appended to a comment written in an online forum, IMHO indicates that the writer is aware that they are expressing a debatable view, probably on a subject already under discussion. One of may such shorthands in common use online, especially in discussion forums.

Internet (Upper case I)
The vast collection of interconnected networks that all use the TCP/IP protocols and that evolved from the ARPANET of the late 60's and early 70's. The Internet now (July 1995) connects roughly 60,000 independent networks into a vast global Internet.

Internet (Lower case i)

Any time you connect 2 or more networks together, you have an Internet – as in international or inter-state.

Intranet

A private network inside a company or organisation that uses the same kinds of software that you would find on the public Internet, but that is only for internal use.

As the Internet has become more popular many of the tools used on the Internet are being used in private networks, for example, many companies have world wide web servers that are available only to employees.

IP Number (Internet Protocol Number)

Sometimes called a dotted quad. A unique number consisting of 4 parts separated by dots, e.g. 165.113.245.2 Every machine that is on the Internet has a unique IP number - if a machine does not have an IP number, it is not really on the Internet. Most machines also have one or more Domain Names that are easier for people to remember.

IRC (Internet Relay Chat)

A huge multi-user live chat facility. There are a

Glossary

number of major IRC servers around the world which are linked to each other. Anyone can create a channel and anything that anyone types in a given channel is seen by all others in the channel. Private channels can (and are) created for multi-person conference calls.

ISDN

Integrated Services Digital Network is basically a way to move more data over existing regular phone lines. ISDN is rapidly becoming available to much of the USA and in most markets it is priced very comparably to standard analogue phone circuits. It can provide speeds of roughly 128,000 bits-per-second over regular phone lines. In practice, most people will be limited to 56,000 or 64,000 bits-per-second.

ISP (Internet Service Provider)

This is an institution that provides access to the Internet in some form, usually for money.

Java

A network-oriented programming language invented by Sun Microsystems that is specifically designed for writing programs that can be safely downloaded to your computer through the Internet and immediately run without fear of viruses or other harm to your computer or files. Using small Java programs (called "Applets"), World wide web pages can include functions such as animations, calculators, and other fancy tricks. We can expect to see a huge variety of features added to the World wide web using Java, since you can write a Java program to do almost anything a regular computer program can do, and then include that Java program in a World wide web page.

JavaScript

JavaScript is a programming language that is mostly used in world wide web pages, usually to add features that make the world wide web page more interactive. When JavaScript is included in an HTML file it relies upon the browser to interpret the JavaScript. When JavaScript is combined with Cascading Style Sheets (CSS), and later versions of HTML (4.0 and later) the result is often called DHTML. JavaScript was invented by Netscape and was going to be called "LiveScript", but the name was changed to JavaScript to cash in on the popularity of Java. JavaScript and Java are two different programming languages.

Glossary

JDK
Java Development Kit, which is a software development package from Sun Microsystems that implements the basic set of tools needed to write, test and debug Java applications and applets.

JPEG (Joint Photographic Experts Group)
JPEG is most commonly mentioned as a format for image files. JPEG format is preferred to the GIF format for photographic images as opposed to line art or simple logo art.

Kilobyte
A thousand bytes. Is actually usually 1024bytes.

LAN (Local Area Network)
A computer network limited to the immediate area, usually the same building or floor of a building.

Leased Line
Refers to a phone line that is rented for exclusive 24-hour, 7-days-a-week use from your location to another location. The highest speed data connections require a leased line.

Listserv
The most common kind of mail list, "Listserv" is a

registered trademark of L-Soft international, Inc. Listservs originated on BITNET but they are now common on the Internet.

Login

noun The account name used to gain access to a computer system. Not a secret (contrast with Password).

verb The act of entering into a computer system, e.g. Login to the WELL and then go to the GBN conference.

Mail list or Mailing List

A (usually automated) system that allows people to send e-mail to one address, whereupon their message is copied and sent to all of the other subscribers to the mail list. In this way, people who have many different kinds of e-mail access can participate in discussions together.

Megabyte

A million bytes. Actually, technically, 1024 kilobytes.

MIME (Multipurpose Internet Mail Extensions)

The standard for attaching non-text files to standard Internet mail messages. Non-text files include graphics, spreadsheets, formatted word-processor documents, sound files, etc.. An e-mail program is said to be MIME Compliant if it can both send and receive files using the MIME standard. When non-text files are sent using the MIME standard they are converted (encoded) into text - although the resulting text is not really readable. Generally speaking the MIME standard is a way of specifying both the type of file being sent (e.g. a Quicktime video file), and the method that should be used to turn it back into its original form. Besides e-mail software, the MIME standard is also universally used by World wide web Servers to identify the files they are sending to World wide web Clients, in this way new file formats can be accommodated simply by updating the Browsers' list of pairs of MIME-Types and appropriate software for handling each type.

Mirror

"To mirror" is to maintain an exact copy of something. Probably the most common use of the term on the Internet refers to "mirror sites" which are world wide web sites, or FTP sites that maintain exact copies of material originated at another location, usually in order to provide more widespread access to the resource. Another common use of the term "mirror" refers to an arrangement where information is written to more than one hard disk simultaneously, so that if one disk fails, the computer keeps on working without losing anything.

Modem (MOdulator, DEModulator)
A device that you connect to your computer and to a phone line, that allows the computer to talk to other computers through the phone system. Basically, modems do for computers what a telephone does for humans.

MOO (Mud, Object Oriented)
One of several kinds of multi-user role-playing environments, so far only text-based.

Mosaic
The first WWW browser that was available for the Macintosh, Windows, and UNIX all with the same interface. Mosaic really started the popularity of the World wide web. The source-code to Mosaic has been licensed by several companies and there are several other pieces of software as good or better than Mosaic, most notably, Netscape.

MUD (Multi-User Dungeon or Dimension)
A (usually text-based) multi-user simulation

Glossary

environment. Some are purely for fun and flirting, others are used for serious software development, or education purposes and all that lies in between. A significant feature of most MUDs is that users can create things that stay after they leave and which other users can interact with in their absence, thus allowing a world to be built gradually and collectively.

MUSE (Multi-User Simulated Environment)
One kind of MUD – usually with little or no violence.

Netiquette
The etiquette on the Internet.

Netizen
Derived from the term citizen, referring to a citizen of the Internet, or someone who uses networked resources. The term connotes civic responsibility and participation.

Netscape
A WWW Browser and the name of a company. The Netscape browser was originally based on the Mosaic program developed at the National Centre for Supercomputing Applications (NCSA). Netscape has grown in features rapidly and is

widely recognised as the best and most popular world wide web browser. Netscape corporation also produces world wide web server software. Netscape provided major improvements in speed and interface over other browsers, and has also engendered debate by creating new elements for the HTML language used by World wide web pages – but the Netscape extensions to HTML are not universally supported.

Network

Any time you connect two or more computers together so that they can share resources, you have a computer network. Connect two or more networks together and you have an Internet.

News group

The name for discussion groups on USENET.

NIC (Networked Information Centre)

Generally, any office that handles information for a network. The most famous of these on the Internet is the InterNIC, which is where new domain names are registered. Another definition: NIC also refers to Network Interface Card which plugs into a computer and adapts the network interface to the appropriate standard. ISA, PCI, and PCMCIA cards are all examples of NICs.

Glossary

NNTP (Network News Transport Protocol)
The protocol used by client and server software to carry USENET postings back and forth over a TCP/IP network. If you are using any of the more common software such as Netscape, Nuntius, Internet Explorer, etc.. to participate in news groups then you are benefiting from an NNTP connection.

Node
Any single computer connected to a network.

Packet Switching
The method used to move data around on the Internet. In packet switching, all the data coming out of a machine is broken up into chunks, each chunk has the address of where it came from and where it is going. This enables chunks of data from many different sources to co-mingle on the same lines, and be sorted and directed to different routes by special machines along the way. This way many people can use the same lines at the same time.

Password
A code used to gain access to a locked system. Good passwords contain letters and non-letters and are not simple combinations such as virtue7.

A good password might be Hot£1-6

Plug-in

A (usually small) piece of software that adds features to a larger piece of software. Common examples are plug-ins for the Netscape browser and world wide web server. The idea behind plug-in's is that a small piece of software is loaded into memory by the larger program, adding a new feature, and that users need only install the few plug-ins that they need, out of a much larger pool of possibilities. Plug-ins are usually created by people other than the publishers of the software the plug-in works with.

POP (Point of Presence, also Post Office Protocol)

Two commonly used meanings: Point of Presence and Post Office Protocol. A Point of Presence usually means a city or location where a network can be connected to, often with dial up phone lines. So if an Internet company says they will soon have a POP in London, it means that they will soon have a local phone number in London and/or a place where leased lines can connect to their network. A second meaning, Post Office Protocol refers to the way e-mail software such as Eudora gets mail from a mail server. When you obtain a SLIP, PPP, or shell account you almost always get a POP account with it, and it is this POP account that you tell your e-mail software to use to get your mail.

Port

First and most generally, a place where information goes into or out of a computer, or both. E.g. the serial port on a personal computer is where a modem would be connected.

On the Internet port often refers to a number that is part of a URL, appearing after a colon (:) right after the domain name. Every service on an Internet server listens on a particular port number on that server. Most services have standard port numbers, e.g. World wide web servers normally listen on port 80. Services can also listen on non-standard ports, in which case the port number must be specified in a URL when accessing the server, so you might see a URL of the form gopher://peg.cwis.uci.edu:7000/ shows a gopher server running on a non-standard port (the standard gopher port is 70).

Finally, port also refers to translating a piece of software to bring it from one type of computer system to another, e.g. to translate a Windows program so that is will run on a Macintosh.

Portal

Usually used as a marketing term to described a World wide web site that is or is intended to be the first place people see when using the World wide web. Typically a "Portal site" has a catalogue of world wide web sites, a search engine, or both. A Portal site may also offer e-mail and other service to entice people to use that site as their main "point of entry" (hence "portal") to the World wide web.

Posting

A single message entered into a network communications system e.g. A single message posted to a news group or message board.

PPP (Point to Point Protocol)

Most well known as a protocol that allows a computer to use a regular telephone line and a modem to make TCP/IP connections and thus be really and truly on the Internet.

PSTN (Public Switched Telephone Network)

The regular old-fashioned telephone system.

RFC (Request For Comments)

The name of the result and the process for creating a standard on the Internet. New standards are proposed and published on line, as a Request For Comments. The Internet Engineering Task Force is a consensus-building body that facilitates discussion, and eventually a new standard is established, but the reference number/name for the standard retains the acronym RFC, e.g. the official standard for e-mail is RFC 822.

Router

A special-purpose computer (or software package) that handles the connection between 2 or more networks. Routers spend all their time looking at the destination addresses of the packets passing through them and deciding which route to send them on.

Security Certificate

A chunk of information (often stored as a text file) that is used by the SSL protocol to establish a secure connection. Security Certificates contain information about who it belongs to, who it was issued by, a unique serial number or other unique identification, valid dates, and an encrypted "fingerprint" that can be used to verify the contents of the certificate. In order for an SSL connection to be created both sides must have a valid Security Certificate.

Server

A computer, or a software package, that provides a specific kind of service to client software running on other computers. The term can refer to a particular piece of software, such as a WWW server, or to the machine on which the software is running, e.g. Our mail server is down today, that's why e-mail isn't getting out. A single server machine could have several different server software packages running on it, thus providing many different servers to clients on the network.

SLIP (Serial Line Internet Protocol)

A standard for using a regular telephone line (a serial line) and a modem to connect a computer as a real Internet site. SLIP is gradually being replaced by PPP.

SMDS (Switched Multimegabit Data Service)

A new standard for very high-speed data transfer.

SMTP (Simple Mail Transfer Protocol)

The main protocol used to send electronic mail on the Internet. SMTP consists of a set of rules for how a program sending mail and a program receiving mail should interact. Almost all Internet e-mail is sent and received by clients and servers using SMTP, thus if one wanted to set up an e-mail server on the Internet one would look for e-mail server software that supports SMTP.

SNMP (Simple Network Management Protocol)
A set of standards for communication with devices connected to a TCP/IP network. Examples of these devices include routers, hubs, and switches. A device is said to be "SNMP compatible" if it can be monitored and/or controlled using SNMP messages. SNMP messages are known as "PDU's" – Protocol Data Units. Devices that are SNMP compatible contain SNMP "agent" software to receive, send, and act upon SNMP messages. Software for managing devices via SNMP are available for every kind of commonly used computer and are often bundled along with the device they are designed to manage. Some SNMP software is designed to handle a wide variety of devices.

Spam (or Spamming)
An inappropriate attempt to use a mailing list, or USENET or other networked communications facility as if it was a broadcast medium (which it is not) by sending the same message to a large number of people who didn't ask for it. The term probably comes from a famous Monty Python sketch which featured the word spam repeated

over and over. The term may also have come from someone's low opinion of the food product with the same name, which is generally perceived as a generic content-free waste of resources.

SQL (Structured Query Language)

A specialised programming language for sending queries to databases. Most industrial-strength and many smaller database applications can be addressed using SQL. Each specific application will have its own version of SQL implementing features unique to that application, but all SQL-capable databases support a common subset of SQL.

SSL (Secure Sockets Layer)

A protocol designed by Netscape Communications to enable encrypted, authenticated communications across the Internet. SSL used mostly (but not exclusively) in communications between world wide web browsers and world wide web servers. URL's that begin with "https" indicate that an SSL connection will be used. SSL provides 3 important things: Privacy, Authentication, and Message Integrity. In an SSL connection each side of the connection must have a Security Certificate, which each side's software sends to

Glossary

the other. Each side then encrypts what it sends using information from both its own and the other side's Certificate, ensuring that only the intended recipient can decrypt it, and that the other side can be sure the data came from the place it claims to have come from, and that the message has not been tampered with.

Sysop (System Operator)

Anyone responsible for the physical operations of a computer system or network resource. A System Administrator decides how often backups and maintenance should be performed and the System Operator performs those tasks.

T-1

A leased-line connection capable of carrying data at 1,544,000 bits-per-second. At maximum theoretical capacity, a T-1 line could move a megabyte in less than 10 seconds. That is still not fast enough for full-screen, full-motion video, for which you need at least 10,000,000 bits-per-second. T-1 is the fastest speed commonly used to connect networks to the Internet.

T-3

A leased-line connection capable of carrying data at 44,736,000 bits-per-second. This is more than enough to do full-screen, full-motion video.

TCP/IP (Transmission Control Protocol/Internet Protocol)

This is the suite of protocols that defines the Internet. Originally designed for the UNIX operating system, TCP/IP software is now available for every major kind of computer operating system. To be truly on the Internet, your computer must have TCP/IP software.

Telnet

The command and program used to login from one Internet site to another. The telnet command/program gets you to the login: prompt of another host.

Terabyte

1000 gigabytes.

Terminal

A device that allows you to send commands to a computer somewhere else. At a minimum, this usually means a keyboard and a display screen and some simple circuitry. Usually you will use terminal software in a personal computer – the software pretends to be (emulates) a physical terminal and allows you to type commands to a computer somewhere else.

Terminal Server

A special purpose computer that has places to plug in many modems on one side, and a connection to a LAN or host machine on the other side. Thus the terminal server does the work of answering the calls and passes the connections on to the appropriate node. Most terminal servers can provide PPP or SLIP services if connected to the Internet.

UDP (User Datagram Protocol)

One of the protocols for data transfer that is part of the TCP/IP suite of protocols. UDP is a "stateless" protocol in that UDP makes no provision for acknowledgement of packets received.

UNIX

A computer operating system (the basic software running on a computer, underneath things like word processors and spreadsheets). UNIX is designed to be used by many people at the same time (it is multi-user) and has TCP/IP built-in. It is the most common operating system for servers on the Internet.

URL (Uniform Resource Locator)
The standard way to give the address of any resource on the Internet that is part of the World wide web (WWW). A URL looks like this: http://www.bbc.co.uk/sport.html or telnet://well.sf.ca.us or news:new.newusers.questions etc.. The most common way to use a URL is to enter into a WWW browser program, such as Netscape, or Lynx.

USENET
A world-wide system of discussion groups, with comments passed among hundreds of thousands of machines. Not all USENET machines are on the Internet, maybe half. USENET is completely decentralised, with over 10,000 discussion areas, called news groups.

UUENCODE (Unix to Unix Encoding)
A method for converting files from Binary to ASCII (text) so that they can be sent across the Internet via e-mail.

Veronica (Very Easy Rodent Oriented Net-wide Index to Computerised Archives)
Developed at the University of Nevada, Veronica is a constantly updated database of the names of

almost every menu item on thousands of gopher servers. The Veronica database can be searched from most major gopher menus

VPN (Virtual Private Network)
Usually refers to a network in which some of the parts are connected using the public Internet, but the data sent across the Internet is encrypted, so the entire network is "virtually" private. A typical example would be a company network where there are two offices in different cities. Using the Internet the two offices merge their networks into one network, but encrypt traffic that uses the Internet link.

WAIS (Wide Area Information Servers)
A commercial software package that allows the indexing of huge quantities of information, and then making those indices searchable across networks such as the Internet. A prominent feature of WAIS is that the search results are ranked (scored) according to how relevant the hits are, and that subsequent searches can find more stuff like that last batch and thus refine the search process.

WAN (Wide Area Network)
Any Internet or network that covers an area larger

than a single building or campus.

WWW (World wide web)

This term is frequently used (incorrectly) when referring to "The Internet", WWW has two major meanings. First, loosely used: the whole constellation of resources that can be accessed using Gopher, FTP, HTTP, telnet, USENET, WAIS and some other tools. Second, the universe of hypertext servers (HTTP servers) which are the servers that allow text, graphics, sound files, etc.. to be mixed together

What is 'screen resolution'?

Sometimes you may come across messages on world wide web sites which say something like "This page is best viewed at a screen resolution of 800x600". You might have wondered what this means. Well, the numbers refer to the number of pixels, or small coloured dots, which are on your screen. There are three main resolutions people usually choose from. The first is 640x480 (used by about 10% of users), then 1024x768 (also used by about 10% of users), and finally 800x600 (the other 80%). Sometimes world wide web sites are designed for a particular kind of resolution, and although you'll still be able to see them in a different resolution, they might not look quite right, or even fit on your screen. With a lower resolution screen (640x480, for example) the pixels will be larger, and so words, pictures and icons will all appear larger than they should be. This is useful if your eyesight isn't perfect). With a high resolution screen (1024x768) the pixels will be very small, and so everything on your screen will be quite tiny. It is therefore useful to know how to change your screen's resolution. It's actually fairly simple. Firstly, right click on your mouse and then select Properties. This will then open up the Display Properties window.

CHAPTER 15
Frequently asked questions

How do I choose a modem?
There is a whole section of the book dedicated to modems, but I'll summarise the basic needs here too. Firstly, there are in fact more ways to connect to the Internet than a modem. Basically, a telephone cable is used to send information between you and the rest of the world, but there's a problem with this. The problem is that telephone cables can only send information in analogue form, but computers deal with information in digital form. A modem then interprets the information between these two forms. However, there are now phone lines which work digitally, so there is no need for a modem to act as an interpreter. These new lines are known as ISDN, (Integrated Services Digital Network), and you can ask your telephone provider about them if you are interested. The advantage of ISDN is that it's much quicker, and there is no connection time, meaning

that you can't get cut off so easily, and that you are charged less. If you are going to have a more traditional connection, then decide whether you want an internal or external modem. Basically, an internal modem will be fitted into a slot in the back of your computer and it will save you desk space. As far as speed is concerned, it is always best to go for a faster modem because it will save your phone bill. Currently a 56k modem is best, but ask your retailer for advice on this, and on fitting if you aren't sure – it is their job to help you.

What do I do if a web page won't open or the computer freezes?
This can and often will happen for a number of reasons, and there are a number of things to try in a recommended order. It is true that the "information Superhighway" has been termed the "Information Footpath" because it can be so slow. This is usually either because the page you're opening has a huge amount of information on it, or the Internet is being used by a huge number of people at that time. If it doesn't seem to be doing anything however, it is best to firstly try clicking on the "Stop" button at the top of your screen on the tool bar and then click on "Refresh". This can sometimes work with more stubborn web pages. If this doesn't work, you should

Frequently asked questions

then check the picture in the very top right corner of your screen. It may appear as a small globe, window symbol or something else, but the important thing to notice is whether it is moving or not. If it is moving , then it is connected to the Internet and is trying to do something. If it is not moving, then what you see on your screen is as far as you will get unless you do something. The next thing to try to use the "Back" button at the top of your screen. This may help to get you back to the last working page you saw. If even this doesn't work, however, click once on the button on your task bar which represents the page you're on. Now try using the buttons at the top of your screen again - Back, Refresh or Home. If you still have no luck, try closing the screen by clicking on the cross in the very top right corner. If none of this helps, simultaneously Control+Alt+Delete and you will be given a list of programs which are currently running on your system. Click on an which say "...Not Responding" and then choose to "End Task". After a few seconds a confirmation box will appear asking if you really do want to end task, and simply choose "End Task" again.

What do I do if I get an error message?
There are many different reasons for error messages, but basically, the tip is to read the message, and

decide if it makes sense. If the message tells you the page you're looking for can't be found, then that makes sense - it happens a lot unfortunately. Just use the Back button and try somewhere else. If the message tells you that an error has occurred, and would you like to continue running scripts on the page, click on Yes - you won't see all the page though. If the message tells you that an illegal operation has occurred, t simply means that two programs are trying to use the same part of the computer's memory at the same time. Although this shouldn't really happen too often, it actually does. In this case, click on Close, but you'll probably find the program closes and you'll lose any unsaved information. If it happens a lot, try to work out when it does happen, and contact the manufacturer if it is the same task that keeps causing the fault. With any other error message, you should simply try to use a different world wide web page if there doesn't seem to be a way of seeing the one you want.

What is a virus and is my computer at risk?
A computer virus is a small program which has been written by someone who has nothing more exciting to do than to try to damage other people's computers. What these viruses can do varies hugely, depending on what they are AIMING to do. The

Frequently asked questions

most harmless ones may just flash up an annoying message, or change a few settings somewhere. The worst kind can actually delete your work and anything that is saved to your hard disk, and can delete your programs so that the computer won't do anything at all. These kinds are not too common fortunately. You are always at risk when you are using a computer which is connected to the Internet, but there are a few things you can do to protect yourself. Firstly, you should invest in an anti-virus protection software package. Secondly, never ever open an e-mail from someone that you don't know. Thirdly, most definitely do not open an attachment in an e-mail from someone you don't know.

How can I protect against a virus?
There are a few things you can do to protect yourself, although none of them can offer a complete guarantee unfortunately. Firstly, you must invest in an anti-virus protection software package, such as Norton Anti Virus. Secondly, as above, never open an e-mail from someone that you don't know. Thirdly, most definitely do not open an attachment in an e-mail from someone you don't know. It is also worth mentioning that some viruses even appear in the form of an attachment that was not in the original e-mail when it was sent. So it is always best to be

cautious as far as attachments go. Obviously common sense helps, such as not downloading programs from people you don't know, or from world wide web sites that aren't known software suppliers you can trust. Also, check any disk, floppy, CD or DVD that you put in your computer for viruses - the software package will have a feature to do this - because that's another common way for viruses to be spread.

Problems solved
Solved! What do I do if…?

…my search returns hundreds of possible links?
This is possibly because you have typed only one term and it was a fairly vague or common word. Try to think of some synonyms and then try adding at least two more specific terms to your search to narrow down the results that you are given.

…my search returns too few documents?
This is the opposite of the previous problem, and may have happened because you are probably searching in the wrong place or you have used too many words, making your search too narrow. Another possibility is that you maybe didn't

Frequently asked questions

configure your search correctly. It is also possible that the information you are looking for is not on the world wide web at all, if it is a specialist subject, for example. In this case, try deleting some of your search words and try your search on another engine, meta searcher, directory, people search, or speciality resource.

...my search returns a "404' – file not found' message?
This message generally appears to tell you that the file you are trying to link to has been moved, removed, or renamed. You should go back to the search engine and do a phrase search or a field search on the title (see these chapters to find out more specifics). You could also try shortening the URL to see if the file might still be on the same server.

...my search returns a 'server does not have a DNS entry' message?
This message is there to tell you that your browser is not able to locate the server (i.e. the computer that hosts the world wide web page). It could mean that the network is busy or that the server has been removed or taken down for maintenance. Firstly, check your spelling and if this does not work, try

again at a different time when the web should have less users.

…my search returns a 'server error' or 'server is busy' message?
This will be the message you see if the server you are attempting to contact is maybe off-line, may have crashed, or may be very busy. Try again at a later time.

…I can't find the home page for a well known product or organisation?
In this case, it is actually worth trying to guess, experimenting with different top-level domain names by using the name, brief name, or the acronym. Many organisations use one of these in their URL. For example, DELL for Dell Computers, or BMA for British Medical Association.
Please not, however, that this does not always work. This may be because another organisation or individual has used the acronym before the well-known company had a chance to use it. The final thing you should try in this case is if your browser is a recent Netscape upgrade, type in the word or phrase without anything else and, if Netscape can, it will match it and take you to the site automatically.

Chapter 16
Useful Websites

The following sites are a good starting point to get an idea of how to find your way around the web. They are well put together and offer good services and products. Just remember, if you buy anything over the internet, make sure you only give payment details across a secure server, or anyone could access your credit/debit card details.

www.amazon.co.uk – a site where you can buy online a huge selection of books, videos, DVDs and games at very reasonable prices.

www.askjeeves.co.uk – a type of search engine, but it works slightly differently – you input a question, rather than simply typing key words.

www.barbie.co.uk – the site dedicated to the doll, there are plenty games for the children.

www.bbc.co.uk – the main BBC site, offering information on their TV and radio programmes.

www.bol.co.uk – a similar site to Amazon.

www.britannica.com – Encyclopaedia Britannica site.

www.btphonet.co.uk – the UK directory enquiries site and will allow you to find someone's phone number by typing in their name and address.

www.dictionary.com – self explanatory.

www.disney.co.uk – the UK site for Disney, offering information on cartoons, news and plenty of games!

www.thesaurus.com – self explanatory.

www.webrewards.co.uk – allows you to send free mobile phone text messages, while building up points which gives a discount on other web pages.

www.yell.com – this is the UK Yellow Pages site.

www.yoox.com – a site which sells most big designer labels at 50% off the high street price.